BUILDING YOUR
NEW TESTAMENT GREEK
VOCABULARY

SOCIETY OF BIBLICAL LITERATURE
Resources for Biblical Study

Edited by
Beverly Gaventa

Number 40
BUILDING YOUR
NEW TESTAMENT GREEK
VOCABULARY
Second Edition

by
Robert E. Van Voorst

BUILDING YOUR
NEW TESTAMENT GREEK
VOCABULARY
Second Edition

by
Robert E. Van Voorst

Society of Biblical Literature
Resources for Biblical Study

Scholars Press
Atlanta, Georgia

BUILDING YOUR
NEW TESTAMENT GREEK
VOCABULARY
Second Edition

by
Robert E. Van Voorst

Library of Congress Cataloging-in-Publication Data
Van Voorst, Robert E.
   Building your New Testament Greek vocabulary / by Robert E. Van
Voorst. —2nd ed.
      p.   cm. — (Resources for biblical study ; no. 40)
   Includes bibliographical references and index.
   ISBN 0-7885-0552-1 (pbk. : acid-free paper)
   1. Greek language, Biblical—Vocabulary. 2. Bible. N.T.—
Language, style. I. Title. II. Series.
PA863.V36   1999
487'.4—dc21   99-28863
                                              CIP

Printed in the United States of America
on acid-free paper

To My Father
Robert Van Voorst

To the Memory of My Mother
Donna Van Voorst

Ἐν ὅλῃ καρδίᾳ δόξασον τὸν πατέρα σου καὶ μητέρα·
τὶ ἀνταποδώσεις αὐτοῖς καθὼς αὐτοὶ σοί;

Contents

Preface

Learning a Greek vocabulary large enough for rapid reading of the New Testament is a daunting task. While a good knowledge of Greek grammar can be gained in a year of study, New Testament vocabulary typically demands much longer attention. This book seeks to aid in this task by enabling the student to build a vocabulary of New Testament Greek by using the principles of word formation and by drawing on the cognate relationships of most New Testament Greek words.

For more than two generations the best tool for learning the Greek vocabulary of the New Testament has been Bruce M. Metzger's *Lexical Aids for Students of New Testament Greek.* [1] This helpful book has been the standard in its field, and rightly so. Still, *Lexical Aids* has shortcomings. Using its lists of 1067 words organized by frequency in the New Testament, the student sees no cognate relationships between words; most memorization is rote. [2] Metzger does also list 690 words, many in addition to those in the frequency lists, by cognate. But because this cognate list does not include even half the words that are in the frequency list, it is unsuitable for comprehensive vocabulary learning. Moreover, my practice and that of other teachers using *Lexical Aids* has been to assign the frequency lists with some thoroughness, but the cognate list only occasionally. Hence the need for one format combining frequency and cognate, a format that can enable the student to memorize Greek vocabulary as easily as possible and in a pedagogically sound manner.

Building Your New Testament Greek Vocabulary is organized as follows: Part One is a guide to using this book and is directed especially to the student. Part Two is an outline of the basic principles of word building. It should be studied with some care before the student proceeds to the cognate lists in Part Three, as a knowledge of the rudiments of word building will make memorizing vocabulary easier and more effective.

---

[1] 1st ed., 1946; 3d ed., Grand Rapids: Baker, 1998.

[2] Computer software programs for learning biblical Greek vocabulary are also based on frequency.

Each word that appears five or more times in the New Testament appears once in Part Three or Part Four, in Part Three if it has any cognate(s) that also appear five or more times in the New Testament, in Part Four if it does not. The words in Part Three are arranged by cognate families in six sections according to the frequency of the most recurrent word in each family. Each word is given a basic English definition based on New Testament usage, and its frequency in the New Testament is listed. Occasionally a well-known English derivative is given to aid in memorization.[3] The lists in Part Four of those Greek words appearing five or more times in the New Testament without common cognates are also divided into six frequency groups. As in Part Three, basic English definitions and occasional English derivatives are given, and the frequency of each word is listed.

The two sections listing words occurring five to nine times (III.G. and IV.G.) can be left aside by those who want to omit learning words of such low frequency that do not have more common cognates. Also, the frequency of each word in the cognate lists (Part Three) is noted, so that the teacher can assign for study any given frequency of Greek words.

The student should alternate between the corresponding sections of Parts Three and Four until both parts have been completed. As an aid to learning, each frequency section is divided into groups of about 20 to 30 words, which seems to be a good number to learn at one sitting.

Part Five gives helps for verb analysis, including lists of the principal parts of the different types of verb. Part Six lists prepositions, both proper and improper. Part Seven lists conjunctions and adverbs, and Part Eight lists number-words. All of these words appear in Parts Three and Four, but they are presented together again for the benefit of the student.

I have drawn the definitions in Parts Three and Four from the second edition of *A Greek-English Lexicon of the New Testament and Other Early Christian Literature* (hereafter BAGD), keeping closely to the New

---

[3] Metzger also includes a good number of English derivatives in his lists. However, many of these words are unfamiliar to most students, even though they are words that students of Bible and theology should learn (e.g., "hamartiology," "macarism," "thaumaturge"). This use of unfamiliar words violates the pedagogical principle that the unfamiliar (here Greek words) should be learned via the familiar (their English derivatives). I have endeavored to restrict the derivatives to more familiar words.

Testament usage.[4] For counting frequency I have used the *Concordance to the Novum Testamentum Graece*.[5] This concordance is based on the twenty-sixth edition of the Nestle-Aland *Novum Testamentum Graece*,[6] the text (but not the textual apparatus) of which is identical to that of the third edition of the United Bible Societies' *Greek New Testament*.[7] In determining cognate relationships, I have used as final authorities E. Boisacq's *Dictionnaire étymologique de la langue grecque*[8] and H. Frisk's *Griechisches etymologisches Wörterbuch*.[9]

I should like to thank here those who helped this project along in various ways. Professor George Landes of Union Theological Seminary (New York) encouraged and advised me as I began this book; it is patterned somewhat upon his *Student's Vocabulary of Biblical Hebrew Listed according to Frequency and Cognate*.[10] My secretary, Sheran Swank, did a most skillful job of putting the challenging manuscript of the first edition on disk. My student assistant, Jeremy Owens, compiled the original index and read the proofs.

Several people wrote me to offer suggestions for improvement, many of which are incorporated in this second edition. I extend my appreciation to Eugene Boring of Texas Christian University, Francis Gignac of the Catholic University of America, and Richard Carlson of Lutheran Theological Seminary, Gettysburg, for their particularly extensive, careful comments. My thanks also are extended to Professor Beverly Gaventa of Princeton Theological Seminary, editor of the SBL's Resources for Biblical Studies series, for accepting this book for Scholars Press publication. Her peer-review committee made several helpful suggestions for this edition. My student assistant, Daven Oskvig, helped to compile the new material in this edition. While all these have made this a better book, I alone am responsible

---

[4] By W. Bauer; translated and revised by W. F. Arndt, F. W. Gingrich, and F. W. Danker. Chicago: University of Chicago Press, 1979. Copyright © 1957, 1979 by the University of Chicago. All rights reserved. Used by permission.

[5] Third edition. Berlin: DeGruyter, 1987.

[6] Stuttgart: Deutsche Bibelstiftung, 1979

[7] Stuttgart: United Bible Societies, 1983.

[8] Heidelberg: Winter; Paris: Klincksieck, 1938.

[9] Heidelberg: Winter, 1960.

[10] New York: Scribners, 1961; now published by Scholars Press.

for its errors. I would be grateful if those who use this book would continue to be so kind as to share their suggestions for improvement with me.

This edition features, in addition to the correction of several miscellaneous mistakes, the following main additions:

- Many new derivatives
- Helps for verb analysis
- Lists of verbs by type
- A list of prepositions
- A list of particles, especially conjunctions and adverbs

My special thanks go, as always, to my wife, Mary, and our sons, Richard and Nicholas, for their constant love and encouragement that make scholarship a happier task.

The quotation in the dedication is excerpted from Sirach 7:27-28: "With all your heart honor your father and mother; what can you give back to them that equals what they have given to you?"

Robert E. Van Voorst

Part One

Guide to Using This Book

In a year's course of studying Greek grammar, students learn at most several hundred Greek words, usually as a part of each lesson in their textbook. But when they come to read the New Testament they find that this vocabulary is woefully inadequate for reading it with any speed or confidence. Often they spend more time looking up unknown words in the lexicon than directly reading the text itself, and they soon get discouraged. At this point in studying Greek, several hundred other words should be learned, and the more the better.

Building Your New Testament Greek Vocabulary is designed to help the student of New Testament Greek cross that gap by learning all the words that occur five or more times in the New Testament. Such a vocabulary of New Testament Greek is sufficient for rapid, confident reading of the text. Part One is directed especially to the student as a brief guide to using this book to the fullest advantage in building a large vocabulary of Greek.

This book combines the *frequency* method of listing vocabulary (based on the number of times a word occurs in the New Testament) with the *cognate* method (based on word families). Cognates are understood here to be words that are related to each other by their possession of a common element, usually called a stem or root, and that are therefore related in meaning as well. Words that are cognate make up a word family. To take an example from English, the words "believe," "belief," "unbelief," "believable," "believer," etc., are all obviously cognates. They share the root "believ-," and make up a family of words. Words in any language do not grow willy-nilly; they are formed in certain regular patterns, and to know the patterns employed in Greek word building is greatly to simplify the tedious process of memorizing New Testament vocabulary. Therefore, the student should carefully study Part Two, "Basic Principles of Greek Word Building," before proceeding to the word lists.

Each cognate group is organized as follows: Each entry in the group has a Greek word, its English definition, an English derivative where helpful, and a frequency number. The English definition is very basic, and is not at all intended to be comprehensive; for full definitions and nuance, BAGD should be consulted. Where an English derivative is given, it can be used as an aid to memorizing the particular Greek word from which it comes, but can also sometimes be used to remember other words in the cognate group as well. Finally, the frequency number can be noted but need not be remembered. Each cognate group begins with the most frequent word, which is in bold type. The group generally proceeds from there in alphabetical order, but not in a strictly uniform way, because very similar words are kept together for ease in memorization regardless of their alphabetical order.

The frequency lists in Part Four have the same basic entries as the frequency and cognate lists in Part Three: the Greek word, its definition, a derivative where helpful, and the frequency number. The Greek words in this part are not necessarily without any cognates in the New Testament, but those cognates that occur do so less than five times. The frequency lists in Part Four are organized according to the same rates of frequency as the lists in Part Three, and the student should alternate between the corresponding sections of Parts Three and Four.

The New Testament contains 1638 words that occur five or more times, all of which are listed here. (This does not include nouns that are always proper, since they are easily discernible from their Greek form.) Of these 1638 words, about 77% can be placed with cognates also occurring five or more times. If the student omits parts III.G. and IV.G., which list most of the words occurring 5–9 times (those that have not been grouped with more frequent cognates), the percentage of words remaining listed with cognates rises to 85%. That the great majority of New Testament Greek vocabulary can thus be listed and learned together with cognates more than compensates for the disadvantage of having to consult two sets of lists.

Although each student must find a system for learning vocabulary that works well for her or him, these suggestions may be helpful:

(1) Begin by studying the words in this book as they are listed in their word families. Note their relationships to each other as far as these are evident. Take care to distinguish very similar words, which you will see in the cognate lists. Use the margins of the pages to make notes about the words studied.

(2) When learning Greek words, repeat the word aloud several times. Pronouncing and hearing the words will help in memorizing them. Take care to accent the right syllable, and when repeating words keep the accent on this syllable. Not doing so complicates the task.

(3) In addition to saying the words aloud, write them out several times. Write and pronounce them together. The more ways that words are impressed on the memory, the more complete memorization will be.

(4) Note the English derivatives when they are given. The meaning of the English word will be suggestive of the meaning of the Greek word. Learn the Greek word by way of the actual English derivative *before* resorting to other, nonsensical associations with English words.

(5) Some students find flash cards helpful. While commercially printed cards are available, it is best to write out one's own. Keep them in cognate groups, especially at first. Then they can be rearranged as one goes along so that more attention is devoted to new and difficult words.

(6) Words that stubbornly resist memorization—which happens to almost every student, and for no easily discernible reason—can often be learned by memorizing a short, familiar phrase from the Greek New Testament in which these words occur.

(7) Using one's actual knowledge of Greek words and the principles of word formation, the student can often make an intelligent preliminary guess about the meaning of unfamiliar words, especially the words of very low frequency not presented in this book. Such guesses should, of course, be soon checked against the lexicon.

(8) Constant review is essential to work Greek vocabulary from short-term memory into long-term memory.

Part Two

Basic Principles of Greek Word Building

The Greek language builds words in rather regular patterns. To know these patterns is to lighten greatly the chore of memorizing vocabulary, especially when memorizing cognate words. We will consider here only the most basic principles of word formation necessary for learning vocabulary. Those who desire more detail should consult a standard Greek grammar.[1] The two most frequent methods of building words are derivation and composition.

Word Building by Derivation

In derivation suffixes are added to a word stem to form different cognate words. For example, to the stem βασιλ-, which carries the notion of "rule, kingship," is added the nominal suffix -ευς to make βασιλεύς, "king"; the verbal suffix -ευω to make βασιλεύω, "I rule, am king"; and the adjectival suffix -ικος to make βασιλικός, "royal." In the course of this adding of suffixes the final part of the stem often undergoes various changes. The rules that govern these changes will not be discussed here, because students who have had some Greek grammar are already familiar with many of these changes as they appear in other contexts, and at any rate the stem is almost always recognizable.

The charts that follow give the *typical* significance of the most important suffixes used in building the vocabulary of the Greek New Testament. Some uses of suffixes will vary from this typical significance, but most adhere to it. The left-hand column lists the suffixes; suffixes for adjectives are in the

---

[1] For example, H. W. Smyth, *Greek Grammar* (revised edition; Cambridge, MA: Harvard University Press, 1956) 225–54; or F. Blass and A. Debrunner, A *Greek Grammar of the New Testament and Other Early Christian Literature,* ed. R. W. Funk (Chicago: University of Chicago Press, 1961) 58–68. It is interesting to note that Blass-Debrunner-Funk's *Greek Grammar* can give a full discussion of word formation without any discussion of roots. The best treatment, and the one relied on here, is by J. H. Moulton and W. F. Howard, *A Grammar of New Testament Greek,* vol. 2, *Accidence and Word Formation* (Edinburgh: Clark, 1928) 267–410.

nominative case and the masculine gender only, for reasons of space. The middle column gives the typical significance of each suffix. The right-hand column gives well-known words from the New Testament as examples of how particular suffixes join stems to build cognate words.[2]

A. Nominal Suffixes

Suffix	Typical Significance	Example from the New Testament
-ος	person, thing	θεός god, God
-της -τηρ -ευς	person, agent	κριτής judge (cf. κρίνω, I judge) σωτήρ savior (cf. σώζω, I save) βασιλεύς king (cf. βασιλεύω, I am king)
-τις -σις -ια	activity	πίστις faith (cf. πιστεύω, I believe) κρίσις judging (cf. κρίνω) οἰκονομία management, task (cf. οἰκονομέω, I manage)
-μα	result of an activity	γράμμα letter (cf. γράφω, I write)
-ια -σια -συνη -εια	abstraction, quality	σωτηρία salvation (cf. σώζω) ἐκκλησία church (cf. ἐκκαλέω, I call out) δικαιοσύνη righteousness (cf. δικαιόω, I justify) βασιλεία kingdom, rule (cf. βασιλεύω)

---

[2] Although we speak of "building" words from the "stem," note that these stems (which some grammarians call "roots") probably never had any existence apart from the words in their families. Stems or roots are *abstractions* from existing words, made for linguistic purposes. What T. O. Lambdin says about Hebrew roots is applicable to the Greek language: "The root is a grammatical abstraction from [cognate] words and not vice-versa; that is, because a root has no existence apart from its incorporation into words, it leads to a misunderstanding of the nature of language to say that words are derived from the root" *(Introduction to Biblical Hebrew* [New York: Scribners, 1971] 18). If this is recognized, the notion of stems/roots can be used as a valid grammatical construct in studying word formation and learning the vocabulary of the Greek New Testament.

Suffix	Typical Significance	Example from the New Testament
-οτης		νεότης youth, young age (cf. νεανίας, young man)
-ιον -ιδιον	diminution	παιδίον infant (cf. παῖς, child) βιβλαρίδιον little book (cf. βίβλος, book)
-ισκος		νεανίσκος young man, boy (cf. νεανίας)

B. Adjectival Suffixes

Suffix	Typical Significance	Example from the New Testament
-ιος	possession	τίμιος honorable (cf. τιμή, honor)
-ικος	belonging to	πνευματικός spiritual (cf. πνεῦμα, spirit)
-ινος	material, type	σάρκινος made of flesh, fleshly (cf. σάρξ, flesh)
-εος		χρύσεος golden (cf. χρυσίον, gold)
-ος -λος -(α)νος -ρος	no definite meaning beyond a general quality or attribute	καλός good, beautiful τυφλός blind γυμνός naked νεκρός dead

C. Adverbial Suffixes

Suffix	Typical Significance	Example from the New Testament
-ως (by far the most common)	manner	δικαίως justly, righteously (cf. δίκαιος, just)
-θεν	from where	ἐκεῖθεν from there (cf. ἐκεῖ, there)
-ιστί	in what language	Ἑλληνιστί in Greek

6

D. Verbal Suffixes

Suffix	Typical Significance	Example from the New Testament
-ω	state or action	ἄγω I lead
-έω		ποιέω I make, do
-άω		τιμάω I honor
-μι		παρίστημι I am present
-άζω	action	χράζω I cry out
-ίζω		βαπτίζω I baptize
-εύω		δουλεύω I serve (as a slave)
-όω	causation	δουλόω I enslave
-ύνω		αἰσχύνω I make ashamed
-αίνω		λευκαίνω I make white

Word Building by Composition

A compound word is formed by the joining of two or more words. English does not form compounds as readily as did Hellenistic Greek, in which word formation through composition was very common.

The great majority of compound words in the New Testament are compound verbs. Compound verbs have a preposition as their first member and a verb as the second member. The precise nuance that the preposition adds to the verb varies, because the meaning of the preposition is often modified by the verb it joins. In addition to a local force (showing direction), several prepositions also sometimes strengthen or perfect the force of verbs with which they are compounded. English has a few examples of this: "eat" is strengthened in "eat up," "swallow" in "swallow down," etc. The student should be aware, though, that by Hellenistic times some of these perfectives had lost the force they originally may have had. Failure to recognize this when it occurs leads to "overtranslating" the verb. For example, one of the meanings of φιλέω is "I kiss," but the compound verb καταφιλέω does not signify an especially intense kiss. Here (as always) usage is determinative, for which a good lexicon should be consulted. The prepositions most often used as perfectives are: συν-, κατα-, ἀνα-, ἀπο-, and ἐκ-. They are translated in the chart below with "thoroughly" and have their own example on a separate line.

7

A. Compound Verbs with Prepositional Prefixes

Prefix	Typical Significance	Example(s) from the New Testament
ἀνα- (ἀν-)	up, again; thoroughly	ἀναβαίνω I go up, embark ἀναζητέω I search after
ἀντι- (ἀντ-, ἀνθ-)	against, instead of	ἀντιλέγω I object to, oppose
ἀπο- (ἀπ-, ἀφ-)	away from thoroughly	ἀποστέλλω I send away ἀπόλλυμι I destroy
δια- (δι-)	through, between	διέρχομαι I go through
εἰς-	into, in	εἰσάγω I lead into
ἐκ- (ἐξ-)	out of, from; thoroughly	ἐξέρχομαι I go out ἐκζητέω I search out
ἐν- (ἐγ-, ἐμ-)	in, into	ἔνειμι I am in, am inside
ἐπι- (ἐπ-, ἐφ-)	on, upon	ἐπικαλέω I call upon
κατα- (κατ-, καθ-)	down, against; thoroughly	καταβαίνω I go down, disembark κατεσθίω I eat up, devour
μετα- (μετ-, μεθ-)	with, after	μετανοέω I repent (implies change)
παρα- (παρ-)	beside, near	πάρειμι I am near
περι-	round, about	περιτέμνω I circumcise (literally "cut around")
προ-	before (of time or place)	προέρχομαι I go before
προσ-	to; nearby	προσάγω I bring to; I come near
συν- (συγ-, συλ-, συμ-)	with, together; thoroughly	συνάγω I gather together συλλαμβάνω I seize, catch
ὑπερ-	over, above	ὑπεροράω I overlook, neglect
ὑπο-	under	ὑποτάσσω I put under, subject

The meaning that prepositional prefixes contribute to verbs can be illustrated by the many compounds in the New Testament of βάλλω, "I put, place, throw." ἀποβάλλω means "I throw off." ἐκβάλλω is "I throw out," hence "I expel." ἐπιβάλλω means "I lay upon." καταβάλλω means "I throw down," in the middle voice "I found, lay," especially used of laying a foundation. "I put around, clothe" is περιβάλλω. προβάλλω is "I put forward, put out." The meaning of συμβάλλω is not readily apparent; it is "I converse, consider, meet." The parts of this compound are hinted at by BAGD, which suggests that συμ + βαλλω is paralleled by our modern colloquial expression, "get it all together." Finally, ὑπερβάλλω is "I go beyond, surpass, outdo."

B. Compounds with Adverbial Prefixes

Compound words of all types can be formed by prefixing an adverbial particle or an independent adverb to a word or stem. The chief adverbial prefixes used in forming compounds in the New Testament are:

Prefix	Typical Significance	Example(s) from the New Testament
ἀ- (ἀν-) (by far the most common)	not, un-, dis-	ἄδικος unjust ἀπιστέω I disbelieve, am unfaithful
εὐ-	well, good	εὐαγγέλιον good news, gospel εὐεργετέω I do good
δυσ-	hard, un-, mis-	δυσεντέριον dysentery

C. Compound Nouns and Adjectives

Compound nouns and adjectives are also formed by joining two words, one of which is usually a noun. As in word building by derivation, changes often occur in the words joined. In compound nouns and adjectives this change almost always occurs at or near the point of conjunction. Fortunately for the student of Greek vocabulary, the two members of the compound are usually recognizable despite these changes, and we will not look directly at the separate members here. But for understanding compounds of all sorts, each member of the compound must be understood and taken into account. [3]

The two members of compound nouns and adjectives can be viewed as standing in various case relationships with each other. Most obvious is an accusative case relationship, where one member of the compound receives the action of the other as its "direct object":

νομοδιδάσκαλος teacher of the law
παντοκράτωρ ruler of all, hence "the Almighty"
οἰκοδεσπότης ruler of a house
ἀρχισυνάγωγος ruler of a synagogue

A dative case relationship may also be apparent:

εἰδωλόθυτος sacrificed to idols
θεοδίδακτος taught by God

Many compounds show a nominative case relationship. That is, the members of the compound stand in a predicate relationship, with the first usually describing the second:

μονογενής unique, only, one-of-a-kind
ἀρχιερεύς chief priest, high priest
ψευδοπροφήτης false prophet

Conclusion

To sum up this treatment of word building, perhaps it would be helpful to offer a rather comprehensive example of word building by both derivation and composition from one root. The root we shall employ is δικ, which in its word family signifies "right, just." Note how this stem joins the prefixes and suffixes listed above to form a whole family of words. (Not all word families are as full and well-formed as this, but this one is highly illustrative of the process.) Nouns formed by derivation and composition are:

δίκη punishment, justice
δικαστής judge
δικαιοσύνη justice, righteousness

---

[3] In the word lists, compound verbs are listed by the second element, the verb. All other compounds are generally listed by the first element.

δικαίωμα righteous deed
δικαίωσις justification, acquittal
ἀδικία unrighteousness
ἀδίκημα sin, crime
ἐκδίκησις retribution, punishment
δικαιοκρισία righteous judgment

Adjectives formed from this root greatly resemble the nouns:

δίκαιος just, righteous
ἄδικος unjust, unrighteous
ὑπόδικος responsible to, answerable to

The verbs of this word family are:

δικαιόω I justify, pronounce righteous
ἀδικέω I wrong, do harm
ἐκδικέω I avenge, punish
καταδικάζω I condemn

Finally, the adverbs are:

δικαίως justly, righteously
ἀδίκως unjustly, unrighteously

Part Three

New Testament Greek Vocabulary Listed by Frequency and Cognate

III. A. Families with One or More Words Occurring 400 or More Times

1. ἀκούω	I hear	(*acou*stic)	430
ἀκοή, -ῆς, ἡ	hearing, ear, report		24
εἰσακούω	I listen to		5
ὑπακούω	I obey		21
ὑπακοή, -ῆς, ἡ	obedience		15

ἀλλά	but, rather, yet		638
ἄλλος, -η, -ο	another, other	(*al*ien)	155
ἀλλήλων	each other, one another		100
ἀλλότριος, -ία, -ον,	belonging to another, strange		14
ἀλλάσσω	I change		6
καταλλάσσω	I reconcile		6

ἄνθρωπος, -ου, ὁ	human being, person	(*anthrop*ology)	551
ἀνθρώπινος, -η -ον	human		7

αὐτός, -ή, -ό	he, she, it; himself, herself, itself; even, very; same	(*auto*mobile)	5601
ἑαυτοῦ, -ῆς, -οῦ	himself, herself, itself		321
ἐξαυτῆς	at once, immediately		6

γίνομαι	I am, become, happen		670
παραγίνομαι	I come, am present		37
γεννάω	I beget		97
γενεά, -ᾶς, ἡ	family, generation	(*genea*logy)	43
γένεσις, -εως, ἡ	beginning	(*genesis*)	5
γένος, -ους, τό	race, stock	(*genus*)	21
γονεῖς, -έων, οἱ	parents		20
μονογενής, -ές	only, unique		9
συγγενής, -ές	related, akin to		9

2. δίδωμι	I give	(cf. *dose*)	415
δῶρον, -ου, τό	gift	(*Doro*thy)	19
δωρεά, -ᾶς, ἡ	gift, bounty		11
δωρεάν	freely		9
ἀποδίδωμι	I give away, give up; I render		48
μεταδίδωμι	I impart, share		5
παραδίδωμι	I hand over, hand down, entrust		119
παράδοσις, -εως, ἡ	handing over, tradition		13

ἐγώ [1]	I	(*ego*)	2666
ἐμός, -ή, -όν	my, mine	(cf. *me, my*)	76
ἐμαυτοῦ, -ῆς	myself		37
ἡμέτερος, -α, -ον	our		8

εἰ	if		507
ἐάν	if		351

εἰμί	I am	(cf. *am*)	2461
ἄπειμι	I am absent		7

[1] The inflected forms of ἐγώ—ἐμοῦ, ἐμοί, etc.—are more clearly cognate to the rest of the words in this group than is ἐγώ.

13

πάρειμι	I am present		24
παρουσία, -ας, ἡ	presence, coming	(*parousia*)	24
ἐξουσία, -ας, ἡ	power, authority		102
ἔξεστι	it is permitted, possible		32
ὄντως	really, certainly, in truth		10
ἔνι	there is (used only after a negative)		6

3. **εἰς**	into, in	(*eis*egesis)	1768
ἔσω	in, inside	(*eso*teric)	9
ἔσωθεν	inside, within; from within		12

ἐκ, before vowels ἐξ	from, out of	(*ex*hale)	916
ἐκτός	outside	(*ecto*plasm)	8
ἔξω	outside, out		63
ἔξωθεν	from the outside, outside		13

ἔρχομαι	I come, go	636
ἀπέρχομαι	I go away	118
διέρχομαι	I go through	43
εἰσέρχομαι	I enter	194
ἐξέρχομαι	I go out, come out	218
ἐπέρχομαι	I come, come upon	9
κατέρχομαι	I come down	16
παρέρχομαι	I go by, (pass.) I pass away	30
προέρχομαι	I go forward, go before	9
προσέρχομαι	I go to, approach	86

4. **ἔχω**	I have, hold	711
ἀνέχομαι	I endure	15
ἀπέχω	I receive; I am distant; I abstain	19
ἐξῆς	on the next day	5
ἐπέχω	I hold fast; I aim at	5

κατέχω	I hold back, hold fast		18
μετέχω	I share, participate in		8
μέτοχος, -ον	sharing in		6
παρέχω	I give, cause		16
προσέχω	I pay attention		24
ὑπερέχω	I surpass		5
ἵνα	in order that, that		663
ἱνατί	why?		6
καί	and, also, likewise		9164
κἀγώ	and I, but I		84
καίπερ	although		5
κἀκεῖ	and there		10
κἀκεῖθεν	and from there		10
κἀκεῖνος, -η, -ο	and that one, and he		22
κἄν	and if, even if, if only		17
κατά	(with gen.) down, against; (with acc.) according to, along	(*cata*lytic)	476
κάτω	below, downward		9
κύριος, -ου, ὁ	master, lord, the Lord	(*Kyrie*)	719
κυριεύω	I am lord, I lord it over		7
5. λέγω	I say, tell	(*leg*end)	2365
λόγος, -ου, ὁ	word, Word	(theo*logy*)	330
λογίζομαι	I reckon, think		41
ἀπολογέομαι	I defend myself		10
ἀπολογία, -ας, ἡ	defense, reply	(*apolog*etics)	8
διαλέγομαι	I discuss, speak	(*dialogue*)	13
διάλεκτος, -ου, ἡ	language	(*dialect*)	6
διαλογίζομαι	I consider, reason		16
διαλογισμός, -οῦ, ὁ	thought, doubt, dispute		14

15

ἐκλέγομαι	I choose, select		22
ἐκλεκτός, -ή, -όν	chosen, select	(*eclec*tic)	22
ἐκλογή, -ῆς, ἡ	election		7
εὐλογέω	I bless		42
εὐλογητός, -ή, -όν	blessed, praised		8
εὐλογία, -ας, ἡ	praise, blessing	(*eulogy*)	16
ὁμολογέω	I confess		26
ὁμολογία	confession		6
ἐξομολογέομαι	I confess		10
προλέγω	I tell beforehand	(*prolog*ue)	15
συλλέγω	I collect		8

μή	not		1043
μηδέ	and not, but not		56
μηδείς, -δεμία, -δέν	no one, nothing		89
μηκέτι	no longer		22
μήποτε	that not, lest		25
μήτε	and not, neither, nor		34
μήτι	(a usually untranslated particle in questions that expect a negative answer)		18

6. **μετά**	(with gen.) with; (with acc.) after, behind	(*meta*physics)	473
μεταξύ	between		9

ὁ, ἡ, τό	the		19904
ὅδε, ἥδε, τόδε	this		10
ὧδε	here		61

ὁράω	I see		449
ὅραμα, -ατος, τό	(a supernatural) vision	(pan*orama*)	12
ἀόρατος, -ον	unseen, invisible		5

ὅς, ἥ, ὅ	who, which, what		1365
οἷος, -α, -ον	of what sort, such as		15
ὅσος, -η, -ον	as great, how great; as far, how far		110
ὅστις, ἥτις, ὅ τι	who, whoever		148
ὅτε	when		103
ὅτι	that, because, since		1297
οὗ	where, whither		54
ὅθεν	from where		15

οὐ, οὐκ, οὐχ	no, not	(*u*topia)	1613
οὐδέ	and not, nor; neither, nor		144
οὐδείς, -εμία, -έν	no one, nothing		227
οὐδέποτε	never		16
οὐκέτι	no more, no longer		47
οὔπω	not yet		26
οὔτε	neither, nor		87
οὐχί	not		53
ἐξουθενέω	I despise, reject		11

---

7. οὗτος, αὕτη, τοῦτο	this		1391
οὕτως	in this manner, thus, so		208

πᾶς, πᾶσα, πᾶν	all, every	(*pan*orama)	1244
ἅπας, -ασα, -αν	all, every		34
πανταχοῦ	everywhere		7
πάντως	certainly		8
παντοκράτωρ, -ου, ἡ	the Almighty		10

πατήρ, πατρός, ὁ	father	(*patr*istics)	414
πατρίς, -ίδος, ἡ	fatherland, hometown	(*patri*ot)	8

17

ποιέω	I do, make		568
περιποίησις, -εως, ἡ	preserving, possessing		5
ποιητής, -οῦ, ὁ	doer, maker	(*poet*)	6
χειροποίητος, -ον	made by human hands		6
ζῳοποιέω	I make alive		11
πολύς, πολλή, πολύ	much, many	(*poly*gamy)	418
πολλάκις	many times, often		18
πρός	(with dat.) near, at; (with acc.) to, toward	(*pros*thetic)	699
ἔμπροσθεν	(adverb) in front, ahead; (prep., with gen.) in front of, before		48
σύ	you		2913
σεαυτοῦ	yourself		43
σός, σή, σόν	your, yours		27
ὑμέτερος, -α, -ον	your		11
τίς, τί	who? which one? what?		555
τις, τι	anyone, anything; someone, something		526
καθότι	as, because		6
ὡς	as, like, so		504
ὡσαύτως	likewise		17
ὡσεί	as, like		21
ὥσπερ	(just) as		36
ὥστε	therefore, so that		83

III. B. Families with One or More Words
Occurring 155–399 Times

1. ἄγγελος, -ου, ὁ   angel, messenger   (*angel*)   176

ἀναγγέλλω	I announce, proclaim		14
ἀπαγγέλλω	I report, proclaim		45
ἐπαγγελία, -ας, ἡ	promise		52
ἐπαγγέλλομαι	I promise		15
εὐαγγελίζομαι	I preach the Good News	(*evangelize*)	54
εὐαγγέλιον, -ου, τό	the Good News, Gospel	(*evangel*ical)	76
καταγγέλλω	I proclaim		18
παραγγέλλω	I command		32
παραγγελία, -ας, ἡ	command		5

ἅγιος, -ια, -ον	holy	233
ἁγιάζω	I make holy, sanctify	28
ἁγιασμός, -οῦ, ὁ	holiness, sanctification	10

ἀδελφός, -οῦ, ὁ	brother	(cf. Phil*adelph*ia)	343
ἀδελφή, -ῆς, ἡ	sister		26

ἁμαρτία, -ας, ἡ	sin	173
ἁμαρτάνω	I sin	43
ἁμαρτωλός, -όν	sinful	47

ἄν	(an untranslatable conditional particle)	167
ὅταν	whenever, when	123

ἀποκρίνομαι	I answer, reply	232
κρίνω	I judge	115
ἀνακρίνω	I question, examine	16
διακρίνω	I differentiate; (mid.) I doubt	19
κατακρίνω	I condemn	18

19

κρίμα, -ατος, τό	judgment, condemnation	(*crime*)	28
κρίσις, -εως, ἡ	judging, judgment	(*crisis*)	47
κριτής, -οῦ, ὁ	judge	(*critic*)	19
ὑπόκρισις, -εως, ἡ	hypocrisy	(*hypocrisy*)	6
ὑποκριτής, -οῦ, ὁ	hypocrite	(*hypocrite*)	18
ἀνυπόκριτος, -ον	genuine, sincere		6

βασιλεία, -ας, ἡ	kingdom, reign		162
βασιλεύς, -έως, ὁ	king		115
βασιλεύω	I rule		21
βασιλικός, -ή, -όν	royal	(*basilica*)	5

2. **γῆ, γῆς, ἡ**	earth	(*geology*)	250
γεωργός, -οῦ, ὁ	farmer	(*George*)	19
ἐπίγειος	earthly		7

γινώσκω	I know	(cf. *know*)	222
γνωρίζω	I make known, reveal		25
γνῶσις, -εως, ἡ	knowledge	(*gnostic*)	29
γνωστός, -ή, -όν	known		15
γνώμη, -ης, ἡ	purpose, opinion		9
ἀναγινώσκω	I read		32
ἀγνοέω	I do not know	(*agno*stic)	22
ἐπιγινώσκω	I know, understand		44
ἐπίγνωσις, -εως, ἡ	knowledge, understanding		20
προγινώσκω	I know beforehand	(cf. *progno*sis)	5

γράφω	I write	(*graph*)	191
γραφή, -ῆς, ἡ	writing		51
γράμμα, -ατος, τό	letter (of the alphabet), writing	(*gramma*r)	14
γραμματεύς, -έως, ὁ	scribe		64

ἐπιγράφω	I write on		5
ἐπιγραφή, -ῆς, ἡ	inscription	(*epigraph*)	5

δόξα, -ης, ἡ	glory, brightness, splendor	(*dox*ology)	166
δοξάζω	I praise, honor, glorify		61
δοκέω	I think, believe; I seem	(*doce*tism)	63
δόγμα, -ατος, τό	decree; doctrine	(*dogma*)	5
δοκιμή, -ῆς, ἡ	character		7
δόκιμος, -ον	approved, genuine		7
ἀδόκιμος, -ον	worthless		8
ἀποδοκιμάζω	I reject		9
εὐδοκέω	I am pleased with		21
εὐδοκία, -ας, ἡ	goodwill, favor		9
συνευδοκέω	I agree with, approve of		6

3. **δύναμαι**	I can	(*dynam*ic)	210
δύναμις, -εως, ἡ	power, strength	(*dynam*ite)	119
δυνατός, -ή, -όν	powerful		32
ἀδύνατος, -ον	powerless		10
ἐνδυναμόω	I strengthen; (pass.) I become strong		7

ἐκεῖνος, -η, -ο	that		265
ἐκεῖ	there, to that place		105
ἐκεῖθεν	from there		37

ἔργον, -ου, τό	work, deed	(*ergo*nomics)	169
ἐργάζομαι	I work, do, accomplish		41
ἐργασία, -ας, ἡ	practice, trade		6
ἐργάτης, -ου, ὁ	workman, doer		16
ἐνέργεια, -ας, ἡ	working, action	(*energy*)	8
ἐνεργέω	I work, produce		21
καταργέω	I make ineffective, abolish		27
κατεργάζομαι	I achieve, bring about		22
λειτουργία, -ας, ἡ	service	(*liturgy*)	6

21

λειτουργός, -οῦ, ὁ	servant	(*liturg*ist)	5
πανουργία, -ας, ἡ	cunning, craftiness, trickery		5
συνεργέω	I cooperate	(*synergy*)	5
συνεργός, -οῦ, ὁ	helper, fellow-worker		13

4. ἐσθίω — I eat — 158

4. ἐσθίω	I eat		158
κατεσθίω	I eat up, devour		15
συνεσθίω	I eat with		5

ἡμέρα, -ας, ἡ	day		389
σήμερον	today		41

θέλω	I wish, will		209
θέλημα, -ατος, τό	will .		62

κόσμος, -ου, ὁ	the world	(*cosmos*)	186
κοσμέω	I adorn, beautify	(*cosme*tic)	10

λαλέω	I speak		296
καταλαλέω	I speak against, slander		5
συλλαλέω	I talk with, discuss		6

λαμβάνω	I take, receive		260
ἀναλαμβάνω	I take up		13
ἀπολαμβάνω	I receive		10
ἐπιλαμβάνομαι	I take hold of, catch		19
καταλαμβάνω	I seize, win		5
μεταλαμβάνω	I receive a share		7
παραλαμβάνω	I take, take with		50
προσλαμβάνομαι	I receive, accept		12
συλλαμβάνω	I seize, I conceive		16
ὑπολαμβάνω	I receive		5

5. μαθητής, -οῦ, ὁ   learner, disciple   (*mathe*matics)   261
μανθάνω   I learn   25

μέγας, -άλη, -α   large, great   (*mega*ton)   243
μεγαλύνω   I make large, magnify   8

μέν   indeed, on the one hand   180
     (but often untranslatable)
μέντοι   though, indeed   8

νόμος, -ου, ὁ   law   (anti*nom*ian)   195
νομίζω   I think, believe   15
νομικός, -ή, -όν   legal; (as a noun) lawyer   9
ἀνομία, -ας, ἡ   lawlessness   15
ἄνομος, -α, -ον   lawless   10

οἶδα   I know   (*idea*)   318
ἰδού   see! behold!   200
ἴδε   see, here is   34
εἴδωλον, -ου, τό   image, idol   (*idol*)   11
εἰδωλόθυτος, -ον   offered to an idol   9
εἰδωλολάτρης,   idolater   (*idolater*)   7
   -ου, ὁ
συνείδησις, -εως, ἡ   conscience   30

---

6. ὄνομα, -ατος, τό   name   (pseudo*nym*)   231
ὀνομάζω   I name   10
εὐώνυμος, -ον[2]   left (as opposed to right)   9

---

[2] Literally, "well-named," a euphemism. The ancient Greeks thought the left hand to be ill-favored.

οὐρανός, -οῦ, ὁ	heaven	(*uran*ium)	274
οὐράνιος, -ον	heavenly		9
ἐπουράνιος, -ον	heavenly		19

πιστεύω	I believe (in), trust		243
πίστις, -εως, ἡ	faith, trust		243
πιστός, -ή, -όν	faithful		67
ἀπιστέω	I disbelieve, am unfaithful		8
ἀπιστία, -ας, ἡ	unfaithfulness, unbelief		11
ἄπιστος, -η, -ον	faithless, unbelieving		23
πείθω	I convince, persuade; I trust in	(cf. *faith*)	52
ἀπειθέω	I disobey, am disobedient		14
ἀπείθεια, -ας, ἡ	disobedience, disbelief		7
ἀπειθής, -ές	disobedient		6

πνεῦμα, -ατος, τό	breath, spirit	(*pneum*onia)	379
πνευματικός, -ή, -όν	spiritual	(*pneuma*tic)	26
πνέω	I blow, breathe		7

7. τότε	then		160
πάντοτε	always		41
τοιοῦτος, -αύτη, -οῦτον	of such a kind, such as this		57
τοσοῦτος, -αύτη, -οῦτον	so great, so far, so much		20

υἱός, -οῦ, ὁ	son		379
υἱοθεσία, -ας, ἡ	adoption		5

ὑπό	(with gen.) by; (with acc.) under	(*hypo*dermic)	220
ὑποκάτω	under		11

χάρις, -ιτος, ἡ	grace, favor	(*charity*)	156
χαίρω	I rejoice, am glad		74
χαρά, -ᾶς, ἡ	joy		59
χαρίζομαι	I give freely, forgive		23
χάρισμα, -ατος, τό	a gift	(*charisma*tic)	17
χάριν	for the sake of		9
εὐχαριστέω	I give thanks		38
εὐχαριστία, -ας, ἡ	thanksgiving	(*Eucharist*)	15
συγχαίρω	I rejoice with		7

III. C. Families With One or More Words
Occurring 100–154 Times

1. ἀγαθός, -ή, -όν	good	(*Agatha*)	102
ἀγαθοποιέω	I do good		9

ἀγαπάω	I love		143
ἀγάπη, -ης, ἡ	love		116
ἀγαπητός, -ή, -όν	beloved, dear		61

αἴρω	I lift up; I take away		101
ἐπαίρω	I lift up, hold up		19

αἰών, -ῶνος, ὁ	age, eternity	(*eon*)	122
αἰώνιος, -ον	eternal		71
ἀεί	always		7

ἀλήθεια, -ας, ἡ	truth, truthfulness		109
ἀληθινός, -ή, -όν	true		28
ἀληθής, -ές	true		26
ἀληθῶς	truly		18

ἀποστέλλω	I send away, send out		132
ἀπόστολος, -ου, ὁ	apostle	(*apostle*)	80
διαστέλλομαι	I order		8
ἐπιστολή, -ῆς, ἡ	letter, epistle	(*epistle*)	24
στολή, -ῆς, ἡ	robe	(*stole*)	9

ἀρχιερεύς, **-έως, ὁ**	high priest, chief priest		122
ἱερεύς, -έως, ὁ	priest	(*hier*archy)	31
ἱερόν, -οῦ, τό	temple		71

2. **ἀφίημι**	I leave, let go, pardon		146
ἄφεσις, -έσεως, ἡ	pardon, forgiveness		17
συνίημι	I understand, comprehend		26
σύνεσις, -εως, ἡ	understanding		7

βάλλω	I throw, place	(*ball*istic)	122
διάβολος, -ου, ὁ	the devil	(*diabol*ical)	36
ἐκβάλλω	I throw out, expel		81
ἐπιβάλλω	I put around, clothe		23
καταβολή, -ῆς, ἡ	foundation		10
λιθοβολέω	I stone		7
παραβολή, -ῆς, ἡ	parable	(*parable*)	50
παρεμβολή, -ῆς, ἡ	camp, army		10
συμβάλλω	I meet, discuss; (mid.) I help		7
ὑπερβολή, -ῆς, ἡ	excess, abundance	(*hyperbole*)	8
ὑπερβάλλω	I surpass		5

βλέπω	I see, look		133
ἀναβλέπω	I look up, gain sight		25
ἐμβλέπω	I look at		12
περιβλέπομαι	I look around		7

δεῖ	it is necessary, one must		101
δέομαι	I ask		22
δέησις, -εως, ἡ	prayer, entreaty		18

δοῦλος, -ου, ὁ	slave		124
δουλεύω	I am a slave, serve		25
δουλόω	I enslave		8
δουλεία, -ας, ἡ	slavery		5
σύνδουλος, -ου, ὁ	fellow-slave		10

δύο	two	(*du*et)	132
δεύτερος, -α, -ον	second	(*Deutero*nomy)	43

3.
ἐγείρω	I raise		144
γρηγορέω	I watch	(*Gregory*)	22
διεγείρω	I wake (someone) up		6

ζάω	I live		140
ζωή, -ῆς, ἡ	life		135
ζῷον, -ου, τό	living thing; animal	(*zoo*)	23

ζητέω	I seek, took for, ask		117
ζήτημα, -ατος, τό	question, issue		5
ζήτησις, -εως, ἡ	investigation		7
ἐκζητέω	I search for		7
ἐπιζητέω	I search for, strive for		13
συζητέω	I discuss, dispute		10

θάνατος, -ου, ὁ	death	(eu*thana*sia)	120
θανατόω	I kill		11
ἀποθνῄσκω	I die		111
θνῄσκω	I die		9
θνητός, -ή, -όν	mortal		6

ἴδιος, -ία, -ον	one's own		114
ἰδιώτης, -ου, ὁ	layman, amateur	(*idiot*)	5

---

4. ἵστημι — I place, set, stand — (*st*and) — 154

ἀνίστημι	I raise, rise, stand up		14
ἀνάστασις, -εως, ἡ	resurrection		42
ἀκαταστασία, -as, ἡ	disturbance		5
ἀνθίστημι	I oppose, resist		14
ἀποκαθίστημι or ἀποκαθιστάνω	I restore, reestablish		8
ἀφίστημι	I go away		14
ἐνίστημι	I have come, am present		7
ἐξίστημι	I am amazed, astonished		17
ἔκστασις, -εως, ἡ	distraction, confusion; trance	(*ecstasy*)	7
ἐπίστασις, -εως, ἡ	pressure, burden		17
ἐφίστημι	I stand by, approach, appear		21
μεθίστημι	I remove		5
παρίστημι	I am present, stand by		41
προΐστημι	I rule, direct; I care for		8
στάσις, -εως, ἡ	uprising, revolt		8
στήκω	I stand, stand firm		10
συνίστημι or συνιστάνω	I present, introduce		16
ὑπόστασις, -εως, ἡ	substantial nature, essence		5

καλέω	I call	(cf. *call*)	148
κλῆσις, -εως, ἡ	calling, position		11
κλητός, -ή, -όν	called, invited		10
ἀνέγκλητος, -ον	blameless, irreproachable		5
ἐγκαλέω	I accuse, charge		7
ἐκκλησία, -as, ἡ	church, congregation	(*ecclesi*astical)	114
ἐπικαλέω	I name; (mid.) I call upon		13

παρακαλέω	I invite; I exhort; I comfort		109
παράκλησις, -εως, ἡ	exhortation, comfort		29
παράκλητος, -ου, ὁ	mediator, helper	(*Paraclete*)	5
προσκαλέομαι	I call, invite		29
συγκαλέω	I call together; (mid.) I summon		8

5. καλός, -ή, -όν	good	(*cal*ligraphy)	101
καλῶς	well, beautifully		37

μένω	I remain, stay	(cf. re*main*)	118
διαμένω	I remain		5
ἐπιμένω	I remain, stay		17
προσμένω	I remain with, stay with		7
ὑπομένω	I remain, endure		17
ὑπομονή -ῆς, ἡ	patience, endurance		32

νῦν	now	(cf. *now*)	148
νυνί[3]	now		20

ὁδός, -οῦ, ἡ	way	(ex*odus*)	101
εἴσοδος, -ου, ἡ	entrance		5

οἶκος, -ου, ὁ	house, dwelling		114
οἰκία, -ας, ἡ	household		94
οἰκέω	I live, inhabit		9
ἐνοικέω	I live in		5
κατοικέω	I live, dwell in		44
οἰκοδεσπότης, -ου, ὁ	the master of the house	(*despot*)	12

[3] An intensive form of νῦν, but with no difference in meaning.

οἰκονομία, -as, ἡ	management; plan	(*economy*)	9
οἰκονόμος, -ου, ὁ	house steward	(*economist*)	10
οἰκουμένη, -ης, ἡ	the inhabited world	(*ecumenical*)	15
οἰκοδομέω	I build		40
οἰκοδομή, -ῆς, ἡ	building, edification; a building		18
ἐποικοδομέω	I build on		7

ὀφθαλμός, -οῦ, ὁ	eye	(*ophthalm*ologist)	100
ἐνώπιον	before		94
μέτωπον, -ου, τό	forehead		8
πρόσωπον, -ου, τό	face		76

---

6. **πορεύομαι**	I go, proceed		154
ἀπορέω	I am in doubt		6
εἰσπορεύομαι	I go in		18
ἐκπορεύομαι	I go out		34
ἔμπορος, -ου, ὁ	merchant	(*empor*ium)	5
παραπορεύομαι	I go by, go through		5

προφήτης, -ου, ὁ	prophet	(*prophet*)	144
προφητεύω	I prophesy		28
προφητεία -as, ἡ	prophecy	(*prophecy*)	19
πρόφασις, -εως, ἡ	pretext, excuse		7
φημί	I say		66
βλασφημέω	I blaspheme	(*blaspheme*)	34
βλασφημία, -as, ἡ	blasphemy	(*blasphemy*)	18

πῶς	how?		103
πώς	somehow		15
ὅπως	(adv.) how; (conj.) that, in order that		53
πόθεν	whence?		29
ποῖος, -a, -ον	of what kind? which? what?		33

ὁποῖος, -ία, -ον	of what sort		5
πόσος, -η, -ον	how great? how much? how many?		27
ποταπός, -ή, -όν	of what sort, of what kind		7
πότε	when?		29
ποτέ	once, formerly		19
πώποτε	ever		6
ποῦ	where?		48

7. | **σάρξ, σαρκός, ἡ** | flesh | (*sarco*phagus) | 147 |
|---|---|---|---|
| σαρκικός, -ή, -όν | fleshly, in the manner of flesh | | 7 |

σῴζω	I save, deliver		107
σωτήρ, -ῆρος, ὁ	savior, deliverer		24
σωτηρία, -ας, ἡ	salvation, deliverance		46
διασῴζω	I save		8

τίθηνι	I put, place	(cf. *theme*)	100
ἀθετέω	I reject		16
ἀνάθεμα, -ατος, τό	object of a curse	(*anathema*)	6
ἀποτίθεμαι	I put off, lay aside		9
διαθήκη, -ης, ἡ	will, testament, covenant		33
διατίθημι	I decree, make a will		7
ἐπιτίθημι	I put upon		39
παρατίθημι	I place beside, place around		19
περιτίθημι	I put around		8
πρόθεσις, -εως, ἡ	presentation; plan		12
προστίθημι	I add		18

φωνή, -ῆς, ἡ	sound, voice	(tele*phone*)	139
φωνέω	I call		43
προσφωνέω	I call at, address		7
συμφωνέω	I agree with	(*symphony*)	6

ψυχή, -ῆς, ἡ	soul	(*psych*iatrist)	103
ψυχικός, -ή, -όν	unspiritual	(*psychic*)	6

III. D. Families With One or More Words
Occurring 50–99 Times

1. ἄγω	I lead	(cf. ped*ag*ogical)	67
ἀνάγω	I lead up		23
ἀπάγω	I lead away		16
εἰσάγω	I lead in		11
ἐξάγω	I lead out		12
κατάγω	I lead down		9
ὁδηγέω	I lead, guide		5
ὁδηγός, -οῦ, ὁ	leader, guide		5
παράγω	I go away, pass by		10
περιάγω	I lead around, go around		6
προάγω	I lead forward, go before		20
προσάγω	I bring, come near		5
συνάγω	I gather together		59
ἐπισυνάγω	I gather together, congregate		8
συναγωγή, -ῆς, ἡ	synagogue	(*synagogue*)	56
ὑπάγω	I go, go away		79

αἰτέω	I ask, ask for	70
αἰτία, -ας, ἡ	cause, reason	20
αἴτιος, -ία, -ον	responsible, guilty	5
παραιτέομαι	I ask for; I refuse	12

ἀνοίγω	I open	77
διανοίγω	I open, explain	8

ἀπόλλυμι	I ruin, destroy	91
ἀπώλεια, -ας, ἡ	destruction	91

2. ἄρχω

ἄρχω	I rule, am first; (mid.) I begin	(olig*arch*)	86
ἀρχή, -ῆς, ἡ	beginning; ruler, authority		55
ἄρχων, -οντος, ὁ	ruler, lord, authority		37
ἀρχαῖος, -α, -ον	ancient, old	(*archaic*)	11
χιλίαρχος, -ου, ὁ	leader of a thousand soldiers, tribune		22
ἑκατοντάρχης, -ου, ὁ	centurion, captain		16
ὑπάρχω	I exist, am present		60
ἀπαρχή, -ῆς, ἡ	first-fruits		9

ἀσπάζομαι	I greet		59
ἀσπασμός, -οῦ, ὁ	greeting		10

βαπτίζω	I baptize	(*baptize*)	77
βάπτισμα, -ατος, τό	baptism	(*baptism*)	19
βαπτιστής, -οῦ, ὁ	baptist, baptizer	(*Baptist*)	12

δαιμόνιον, -ου, τό	demon, evil spirit	(*demon*)	63
δαιμονίζομαι	I am demon-possessed		13

δέχομαι	I take, receive		56
ἀπεκδέχομαι	I await eagerly		8
ἀποδέχομαι	I welcome, receive		7
δεκτός, -ή, -όν	acceptable, welcome		5
προσδοκάω	I wait for		16
ἐκδέχομαι	I expect		6
παραδέχομαι	I receive		6
προσδέχομαι	I receive, welcome; I wait for		14
δεξιός, -ά, -όν	right (as opposed to left)	(cf. *dex*terity)	54
εὐπρόσδεκτος, -ον	acceptable, welcome		5

διδάσκω	I teach	(cf. *dida*ctic)	97
διδάσκαλος, -ου ὁ	teacher		59
διδασκαλία, -as, ἡ	teaching, instruction		21
διδαχή, -ῆς, ἡ	teaching		30

---

3. δικαιοσύνη, -ης, ἡ — righteousness — 92

δίκαιος, -a, -ον	righteous, just	79
δικαιόω	I justify	39
δικαίωμα, -ατος, τό	requirement; righteous deed	10
δικαίως	justly	5
ἀδικέω	I do wrong, treat unjustly	28
ἀδικία, -as, ἡ	wrongdoing, unrighteousness	25
ἄδικος, -ον	unjust	12
ἀντίδικος, -ου, ὁ	opponent	5
ἐκδικέω	I avenge someone	6
ἐκδίκησις, -εως, ἡ	vengeance, punishment	9
καταδικάζω	I condemn	5

| διό | therefore, for this reason | 53 |
| διότι | because, therefore | 23 |

δώδεκα	twelve		75
δέκα	ten	(*dec*ade)	24
δεκατεσσαρες	fourteen		5

| ἐλπίς, -ίδος, ἡ | hope | 53 |
| ἐλπίζω | I hope, hope for | 31 |

ἐντολή, -ῆς, ἡ	commandment, order	67
ἐντέλλομαι	I command, order	15
ἀνατέλλω	I rise up	9
ἀνατολή, -ῆς, ἡ	rising, east	11

ἑπτά	seven		88
ἕβδομος, -η, -ον	seventh		9

ἐρωτάω	I ask, request		63
ἐπερωτάω	I ask (a question)		56

4. εὐθύς

εὐθύς	immediately		51
εὐθύς, -εῖα, -ύ	straight		8
εὐθέως	immediately		36

ἤδη	now, already		61
δή	indeed, now		5

θεωρέω	I see, perceive	(*theory*)	58
θεάομαι	I see, look at	(*theater*)	22

ἱμάτιον, -ου, τό	garment		60
ἱματισμός, -οῦ, ὁ	clothing		5

κακός, -ή, -όν	evil, bad		50
κακία, -ας, ἡ	wickedness, malice		11
κακόω	I harm, mistreat		6
κακῶς	wickedly, badly		16
ἐγκακέω	I become weary, lose heart		6

καρπός, -ου, ὁ	fruit		66
καρποφορέω	I bear fruit		8
ἄκαρπος, -ον	unfruitful		7

κηρύσσω	I proclaim, preach		61
κήρυγμα, -ατος, τό	proclamation, preaching		9

κράζω	I cry, call out		56
ἀνακράζω	I cry out		5

λίθος, -ου, ὁ	stone	(*litho*graphy)	59
λιθάζω	I stone (a person)		9

5.
λοιπός, -ή, -όν	remaining, other		55
λείπω	I lack, fall short		6
ἀπολείπω	I leave (behind); I remain		7
ἐγκαταλείπω	I leave behind, forsake		10
καταλείπω	I leave behind		24

ἀπολύω	I set free, let go, send away	67
λύω	I loose, set free	42
ἀπολύτρωσις, -εως, ἡ	release, redemption	10
ἐκλύομαι	(pass.) I become weary, give out	5
καταλύω	I destroy, abolish	17
παραλύομαι	I am disabled	5
παραλυτικός, -ή, -όν	lame; (as a noun) a paralytic (*paralytic*)	10

μᾶλλον	more, rather	81
μάλιστα	most of all, especially	12

μαρτυρέω	I bear witness, testify		76
μαρτυρία, -ας, ἡ	testimony		37
μαρτύριον, -ου, τό	testimony, proof		19
μαρτύρομαι	I testify, affirm		5
μάρτυς, -τυρος, ὁ	witness	(*martyr*)	35
ψευδομαρτυρέω	I bear false witness		5

μέσος, -η, -ον	middle, in the middle	(*Meso*potamia)	58
μεσίτης, -ου, ὁ	mediator		6

6. παιδίον, -ου, τό | infant, young child | | 52 |

6. παιδίον, -ου, τό	infant, young child		52
παῖς, παιδός, ὁ	child	(*pedi*atrician)	24
παιδίσκη, -ης, ἡ	female slave		13
παιδεία, -ας, ἡ	upbringing, training		6
παιδεύω	I bring up, train		13
ἐμπαίζω	I ridicule, mock		13

πέμπω	I send	79
ἀναπέμπω	I send up	5
μεταπέμπομαι	I send for	9
προπέμπω	I accompany	9

περιπατέω	I go about, walk around	95
πατέω	I tread	5
καταπατέω	I trample under foot	5

πίνω	I drink		73
ποτήριον, -ου, τό	a drink	(*po*table)	31
ποτίζω	I give a drink		15
καταπίνω	I drink down		7

πίπτω	I fall	90
ἀναπίπτω	I lie down, recline	12
ἐκπίπτω	I fall off, fall from	10
ἐμπίπτω	I fall in, fall into	7
ἐπιπίπτω	I fall upon	11
παράπτωμα, -ατος, τό	transgression, sin	20
προσπίπτω	I fall down before, fall upon	8
πτῶμα, -ατος, τό	corpse	7

7. πληρόω	I fill, make full, finish		87
πλήρωμα, -ατος, τό	fullness		17
πλήρης, -ες	full, complete		16
πληθύνω	I increase, multiply		12
πλῆθος, -ους, τό	crowd, multitude	(*pleth*ora)	31
ἀναπληρόω	I fill up		6
πίμπλημι	I fill, fulfill		24
ἐμπίμπλημι	I fill, satisfy		5

πλοῖον, -ου, τό	boat, ship		68
πλοιάριον, -ου, τό	small ship, boat		5
πλέω	I sail		6

πονηρός, -ά, -όν	wicked, bad		78
πονηρία, -ας, ἡ	wickedness, sinfulness		7

πούς, ποδος, ὁ	foot	(*pod*iatrist)	93
ὑποπόδιον, -ου, τό	footstool		7

προσεύχομαι	I pray		86
προσευχή, -ῆς, ἡ	prayer		37
εὔχομαι	I pray		7

πῦρ, πυρός, τό	fire	(*pyre*)	73
πυρετός, -οῦ, ὁ	fever		6
πυρόομαι	I burn, am inflamed		6

ῥῆμα, -ατος, τό	word, saying; thing, matter	(cf. *rhe*toric)	68
παρρησία, -ας, ἡ	openness, confidence		31
παρρησιάζομαι	I speak freely, openly		9

σημεῖον, -ου, τό	sign	(*sema*phore)	77
σημαίνω	I make known, indicate		6

σοφία, -ας, ἡ	wisdom	(philo*sophy*)	51
σοφός, -ή, -όν	wise		20

σπείρω	I sow		52
σπέρμα, -ατος, τό	seed	(*sperm*)	43
σπόρος, -ου, ὁ	seed	(*spore*)	6

8.
τέκνον, -ου, τό	child		99
τεκνίον, -ου, τό	little child		8
τίκτω	I give birth to		18
πρωτότοκος, -ον	first-born		8

τηρέω	I keep, observe		70
παρατηρέω	I watch, observe		6

τρεῖς, τρία	three	(cf. *tri*nity)	67
τρίς	three times		12
τρίτος, -η, -ον	third		56
τριάκοντα	thirty		9

φέρω	I bear, carry	(cf. *fer*tile)	66
ἀναφέρω	I bring up, take up		10
ἀποφέρω	I carry away		6
διαφέρω	I differ, am superior		13
εἰσφέρω	I bring in		8
ἐκφέρω	I carry out, send out		8
πληροφορέω	I fill, fulfill		6
προσφέρω	I bring to, offer		47
προσφορά, -ᾶς, ἡ	offering, gift		9
συμφέρω	I help, am profitable		15

φορέω	I bear, wear		6
φόρος, -ου, ὁ	tribute, tax		5
φορτίον, -ου, τό	burden, load		6

φοβέομαι	I fear		95
φόβος, -ου, ὁ	fear	(*phob*ia)	47
ἔμφοβος, -ον	afraid		5

φῶς, φωτός, τό	light	(*photo*graph)	73
φωτίζω	I illuminate		11
φωτεινός, -ή, -όν	shining, bright		5

III. E. Families With One or More Words
Occurring 26–49 Times

1. **ἀγοράζω**	I buy		30
ἀγορά, -ᾶς, ἡ	marketplace		11

ἀκάθαρτος,	impure, unclean		32
-η, -ον			
ἀκαθαρσία, -ας, ἡ	impurity, immorality		10
καθαρίζω	I make clean, purify	(cf. *cathar*sis)	31
καθαρισμός, -οῦ, ὁ	purification		7
καθαρός, -ά, -όν	clean, pure		27

ἄξιος, -ία, -ον	worthy, fit	(*axi*om)	41
ἀξιόω	I deem worthy		7
ἀξίως	worthily		6

ἀποκαλύπτω	I reveal	(*apocalypt*ic)	26
ἀποκάλυψις, -εως, ἡ	revelation	(*apocalypse*)	18
καλύπτω	I cover, hide		8

| ἀρνέομαι | I deny | | 33 |
| ἀπαρνέομαι | I deny | | 11 |

ἀσθενέω	I am weak, sick		33
ἀσθένεια, -ας, ἡ	weakness		24
ἀσθενής, -ές	weak, powerless		26

| βιβλίον, -ου, τό | book, scroll | (*biblio*graphy) | 34 |
| βίβλος, -ου, ἡ | book | (*Bible*) | 10 |

βούλομαι	I wish, desire	(cf. *vol*ition)	37
βουλή, -ῆς, ἡ	purpose, counsel		12
βουλεύομαι	I resolve, decide		6
συμβούλιον, -ου, τό	plan, purpose		8

2. γαμέω	I marry	(mono*gamy*)	28
γάμος, -ου, ὁ	marriage		16
γαμίζω	I give in marriage		7

δέω	I bind, tie		43
δεσμός, -οῦ, ὁ	bond, fetter		18
δέσμιος, -ου, ὁ	prisoner		16
ὑπόδημα, -ατος, τό	sandal		10

δείκνυμι [4]	I point out, show		33
ἐνδείκνυμι	I show, demonstrate	(*indic*ation)	11
ἐπιδείκνυμι	I show, point out		7

---

[4] This word group is closely related to that δίκη, but for pedagogical purposes it is listed separately.

41

ὑποδείκνυμι	I show, indicate		6
ὑπόδειγμα, -ατος, τό	example, pattern		6

διακονέω	I wait at table, serve		37
διακονία, -ας, ἡ	service		34
διάκονος, -ου, ὁ and ἡ	deacon	(*deacon*)	29

διώκω	I hasten; I pursue, persecute	45
διωγμός, -οῦ, ὁ	persecution	10

ἐγγίζω	I come near	42
ἐγγύς	near	31

ἐλεέω	I have mercy	29
ἔλεος, -ους, τό	mercy, compassion	27
ἐλεημοσύνη, -ης, ἡ	alms	13

3. ἐνδύω	I clothe	(cf. *endue*)	27
ἔνδυμα, -ατος, τό	garment, clothing		8
ἐκδύω	I strip, take off		6
δυσμή, -ῆς, ἡ	going down, west		5

ἐπεί	because, since, for	26
ἐπειδή	since, because	10

ἐπιθυμία, -ας, ἡ	desire, longing	38
ἐπιθυμέω	I desire, long for	16
θυμός, -οῦ, ὁ	anger, wrath	18
ὁμοθυμαδόν	with one mind	11
προθυμία, -ας, ἡ	willingness, goodwill	5

ἐπιστρέφω	I turn, turn around, turn back		36
ἀναστρέφω	I act, live		9
ἀναστροφή, -ῆς, ἡ	way of life, conduct		13
διαστρέφω	I make crooked, pervert		7
στρέφω	I turn, change	(cata*strophe*)	21
ὑποστρέφω	I turn back, return		35

ἔρημος, -ον	empty, deserted; (as a noun [ἡ]) the desert, wilderness	(*hermit*)	48
ἐρημόομαι	(pass.) I am laid waste		5

ἑτοιμάζω	I prepare	40
ἕτοιμος, -η, -ον	prepared	17

ἐχθρός, -ά, -όν	hostile; (as a noun) enemy	32
ἔχθρα, -ας, ἡ	enmity	6

4. ἡγέομαι	I lead, guide; I think		28
ἡγεμών, -όνος, ὁ	governor, procurator	(*hegemony*)	20
διηγέομαι	I tell, relate		8
ἐξηγέομαι	I explain, interpret	(cf. *exege*sis)	6

θαυμάζω	I wonder, marvel	43
θαυμαστός, -ή, -όν	wonderful, marvelous	6

θλῖψις, -εως, ἡ	affliction, tribulation	45
θλίβω	I afflict, oppress	10

θυσία, -ας, ἡ	sacrifice, offering	28
θυσιαστήριον, -ου, τό	altar	23
θύω	I sacrifice	14
θυμίαμα, -ατος, τό	incense, incense offering	6

ἰάομαι	I heal		26
ἰατρός, -οῦ, ὁ	physician	(psychi*atr*ist)	7

ἰσχυρός, -ά, -όν	strong, powerful		29
ἰσχύς, -ύος, ἡ	strength, power		10
ἰσχύω	I am strong, powerful		28

καυχάομαι	I boast, glory	37
καύχημα, -ατος, τό	boast, object of boasting	11
καύχησις, -εως, ἡ	boasting	11

κλαίω	I weep, cry	40
κλαυθμός, -οῦ, ὁ	weeping	9

5. **κρατέω**	I take hold of, hold fast		47
κράτος, -ους, τό	power, rule	(cf. demo*cracy*)	12
κρείττων, -ον and κρείσσων	better		19

λυπέω	I grieve; (pass.) I am sad, grieve	26
λύπη, -ης, ἡ	grief, sorrow, pain	16
περίλυπος, -ον	very sad, deeply sorrowed	5

μέρος, -ους, τό	part	42
μερίζω	I divide, separate	14
διαμερίζω	I distribute	11
μερίς, -ίδος, ἡ	part, share	5

μετανοέω	I repent, am converted		34
μετάνοια, -ας, ἡ	repentance, conversion		22
νοέω	I perceive, understand	(cf. para*n*oia)	14

νόημα, -ατος, τό	thought, mind, design		6
νοῦς, νοός, ὁ	understanding, mind		24
νουθετέω	I admonish, instruct		8
διάνοια, -ας, ἡ	understanding, mind		12
μνημεῖον, **-ου, τό**	grave, tomb		40
μνῆμα, -ατος, τό	grave, tomb		8
μνεία, -ας, ἡ	remembrance, memory	(am*ne*sia)	7
μνημονεύω	I remember, mention		21
ἀναμιμνῄσκω	I remind		6
ὑπομιμνῄσκω	I remind		7
ὅμοιος, -α, -ον	like, similar		45
ὁμοίως	likewise, so, similarly		30
ὁμοιόω	I liken, compare		15
ὁμοίωμα, -ατος, τό	likeness, form		6
6. **ὀπίσω**	behind, back		35
ὄπισθεν	from behind		7
ὀργή, -ῆς, ἡ	anger, indignation		36
ὀργίζομαι	I am angry, indignant		8
ὀφείλω	I owe		35
ὀφειλέτης, -ου, ὁ	debtor		7
πάσχω	I suffer, endure		42
πάθημα, -ατος, τό	suffering	(em*path*y)	16
πειράζω	I test, tempt		38
πειρασμός, -οῦ, ὁ	test, temptation		21

πέντε	five	(*penta*gon)	36
πεντήκοντα	fifty		5
πεντακισχίλιοι	five thousand		6

περισσεύω	I have an abundance, am rich		39
περίσσευμα, -ατος, τό	abundance, fullness		5
περισσός, -ή, -όν	abundant, superfluous		6
περισσότερος, -α, -ον	greater, more		17
περισσοτέρως	far greater, far more, especially		12

περιτομή, -ῆς, ἡ	circumcision		36
περιτέμνω	I circumcise		17

πλανάω	I lead astray, deceive		39
πλάνη, -ης, ἡ	wandering, error, deceit	(*plane*t)	10
πλάνος, -ον	deceitful; (as a noun) deceiver, impostor		5

πλούσιος, -ία, -ον	rich		28
πλοῦτος, -ου, ὁ	riches	(*pluto*cracy)	22
πλουτέω	I am rich, become rich		12

7. **πράσσω**	I do, accomplish		39
πρᾶξις, -εως, ἡ	acting, deed	(*practi*cal)	6
πρᾶγμα, -ατος, τό	deed, thing	(*pragma*tic)	11

πρό	(with gen.) before, in front of	(*pro*logue)	47
πρότερος, -α, -ον	earlier, former	(*proto*type)	11

σκανδαλίζω	I cause to fall	(*scandalize*)	29
σκάνδαλον, -ου, ὁ	that which gives offense, temptation to sin	(*scandal*)	15

σκότος, -ους, τό	darkness	31
σκοτία, -ας, ἡ	darkness	16
σκοτίζομαι	I am/become dark	5

σταυρόω	I crucify	46
σταυρός, -οῦ, ὁ	cross	27
συσταυρόω	I crucify with	5

στρατιώτης, -ου, ὁ	soldier		26
στράτευμα, -ατος, τό	army		8
στρατεύομαι	I serve in the army		7
στρατηγός, -οῦ, ὁ	praetor, captain	(*strategy*)	10

τέλος, -ους, τό	end	40
τελέω	I finish, carry out	28
τέλειος, -α, -ον	complete, perfect	19
τελειόω	I complete, perfect	23
τελευτάω	I die	13
ἐπιτελέω	I end, complete	10
συντελέω	I complete, fulfill	· 6
συντέλεια, -ας, ἡ	completion, close	6

τέσσαρες	four	30
τεσσαράκοντα	forty	15
τέταρτος, -η, -ον	fourth	10
τετρακισχίλιοι	four thousand	5
εἰκοσιτέσσαρες	twenty-four	6

8. τιμή, -ῆs, ἡ | price, value, honor | | 41
τίμιος, -α, -ον | valuable, precious | | 13
τιμάω | I honor | (*Tim*othy) | 21
ἀτιμάζω | I dishonor | | 7
ἀτιμία, -αs, ἡ | dishonor | | 7
ἐπιτιμάω | I rebuke, reprove | | 29
ἔντιμος, -ον | honored, valuable | | 5

ὑποτάσσω	I subject, subordinate		38
τάσσω	I place, order		8
τάξις, -εως, ἡ	order	(syn*tax*)	9
ἀντιτάσσομαι	I oppose		5
ἀποτάσσομαι	I say farewell, leave		6
διατάσσω	I order, direct		16
ἐπιτάσσω	I order		10
ἐπιταγή, -ῆs, ἡ	order		7
προστάσσω	I order		7

φανερόω	I reveal, make known		49
φαίνω	I shine; (mid.) I appear, become visible	(*phan*tom)	31
φανερός, -ά, -όν	visible, clear		18
ἀφανίζω	I make invisible, unrecognizable		5
ἐμφανίζω	I reveal, make known		10
ἐπιφάνεια, -αs, ἡ	appearance, appearing	(*epiphany*)	6

φεύγω	I flee	(*fu*gitive)	29
ἐκφεύγω	I escape		8

φίλος, -η, -ον	beloved, loving; (as a noun) friend	(*philo*sophy)	29
φιλέω	I love, like; I kiss		27
φίλημα, -ατος, τό	a kiss		7
καταφιλέω	I kiss		6
φιλαδελφία, -αs, ἡ	love of brother or sister	(*Philadelphia*, PA)	6

9. φρονέω — I think — 26

φρόνιμος, -ον	sensible, thoughtful	14
ἄφρων, -ον	foolish, ignorant	11
εὐφραίνω	I gladden; (pass.) I am glad	14
καταφρονέω	I despise, scorn	9
σωφρονέω	I am in sound mind	6

φυλακή, -ῆς, ἡ — watch, guard — (prophylactic) — 47

φυλάσσω	I watch, guard	31
γαζοφυλακεῖον, -ου, τό	treasure room, treasury	5

φυλή, -ῆς, ἡ — tribe, nation — (*phylum*) — 31

φύσις, -εως, ἡ	nature	14
φυτεύω	I plant	11

χρεία, -ας, ἡ — need, necessity — 49

χράομαι	I use	11
χρῄζω	I need	5
χρῆμα, -ατος, τό	property, money	6
χρηματίζω	I reveal; I bear a name	9
χρηστός, -ή, -όν	useful	7
χρηστότης, -ητος, ἡ	goodness, usefulness	10
παραχρῆμα	immediately	18

χρόνος, -ου, ὁ — time — (*chro*nicle) — 49

χρονίζω	I take time, delay	5

χώρα, -ας, ἡ — country, land — 28

χωρέω	I make room, give away	10
χωρίον, -ου, τό	place, land, field	10

| χωρίς | without, apart from | 41 |
| χωρίζω | I divide, separate | 13 |

III. F. Families With One or More Words
Occurring 10–25 Times

| 1. ἀγαλλιάω | I exult, am glad | 11 |
| ἀγαλλίασις, -εως, ἡ | exultation, joy | 5 |

| ἀμπελών, -ῶνος, ὁ | vineyard | 23 |
| ἄμπελος, -ου, ἡ | vine | 9 |

ἀνά	(with acc.) up; (with numbers) each, apiece	13
ἄνωθεν	from above, again	13
ἄνω	above, upward	9
ἐπάνω	above, over	19

ἀνάγκη, -ης, ἡ	necessity, distress	18
ἀναγκάζω	I compel	9
ἀναγκαῖος, -α, -ον	necessary	8

ἀναιρέω	I take away, destroy		24
ἀφαιρέω	I take away		10
ἐξαιρέω	I take out; (mid.) I free		8
καθαιρέω	I tear down, destroy		9
αἵρεσις, -εως, ἡ	party, dissension	(*heresy*)	9

| ἀναχωρέω | I go away, take refuge | 14 |
| περίχωρος, -ον | neighboring; (as a noun) neighborhood | 9 |

ἅπαξ	once		14
ἐφάπαξ	once for all		5

ἀργύριον, -ου, τό	silver	(*Arg*entina)	20
ἄργυρος, -ου, τό	silver		5

ἀρέσκω	I please		17
ἀρεστός, -ή, -όν	pleasing		5
εὐάρεστος, -ον	pleasing, acceptable		9

2. ἁρπάζω	I seize, steal		14
ἅρπαξ, -αγος	rapacious; (as a noun) robber		5

ἀστήρ, -έρος, ὁ	star	(*astr*onomy)	24
ἀστραπή, -ῆς, ἡ	lightning		9

βασανίζω	I torture, torment	12
βασανισμός, -οῦ, ὁ	torture, tormenting	6

βοάω	I call, shout	12
βοηθέω	I aid, help	8

βρῶμα, -ατος, τό	food	17
βρῶσις, -εως, ἡ	eating, rust, food	11

γέμω	I am full	11
γεμίζω	I fill	8

γόνυ, -ατος, τό	knee		12
γωνία, -ας, ἡ	corner	(trig*on*ometry)	9

δεῦτε	come (on)!	12
δεῦρο	come, come here	9

ἐκκόπτω	I cut off, cut down	10
ἀποκόπτω	I cut off	6
ἐγκόπτω	I hinder, thwart	5
κόπτω	I cut	8
προκόπτω	I progress	6
προσκόπτω	I take offense at	8
πρόσκομμα, -ατος, τό	stumbling, offense	6

3. ἕκτος, -η, -ον	sixth		14
ἕξ	six	(s*ix*)	10
ἑξήκοντα	sixty		6

ἐλαία, -ας, ἡ	olive tree	13
ἔλαιον, -ου, τό	oil	11

ἐντεῦθεν	from here	10
ἐνθάδε	here	8

ἔπαινος, -ου, ὁ	praise	11
ἐπαινέω	I praise	6
αἰνέω	I praise	8

ἐπαύριον	tomorrow	17
αὔριον	tomorrow	14

ἔπειτα	then		16
εἶτα	then, next		15

ἐπισκέπτομαι	I oversee, care for		11
ἐπίσκοπος, -ου, ὁ	overseer, bishop	(*episcop*al)	5
σκοπέω	I lookout for, notice	(cf. tele*scope*)	6

ἐπιτρέπω	I permit		18
ἐκτρέπομαι	I turn, turn away		5
ἐντρέπω	I shame; (mid.) I respect		9
τρόπος, -ου, ὁ	manner, kind		13

εὐσέβεια, -ας, ἡ	piety, godliness		15
σέβομαι	I worship		10
ἀσέβεια, -ας, ἡ	ungodliness, impiety		6
ἀσεβής, -ές	godless, impious		9

4. ζῆλος, -ου, ὁ and ζῆλος, -ους, τό	zeal, jealousy	(*zeal*)	16
ζηλόω	I am zealous, jealous		11
ζηλωτής, οῦ, ὁ	zealot	(*zealot*)	8

ζύμη, -ης, ἡ	yeast, leaven	(en*zym*e)	13
ἄζυμος, -ον	unleavened		9

θεμέλιος, -ου, ὁ	foundation		15
θεμέλιον, -ου, τό	foundation		11
θεμελιόω	I lay a foundation		5

θερίζω	I harvest		21
θερισμός, -οῦ, ὁ	harvest		13

θησαυρός, -οῦ, ὁ	treasure	(*thesaurus*)	17
θησαυρίζω	I store up		8

καίω	I burn		12
κατακαίω	I burn down, consume		12

καταισχύνω	I put to shame, dishonor		13
αἰσχύνομαι	I am ashamed		5
αἰσχύνη, -ης, ἡ	shame		6
ἐπαισχύνομαι	I am ashamed		11

κατηγορέω	I accuse	(cf. *categori*cal)	23
κατήγορος, -ου, ὁ	accuser		5

κεῖμαι	I lie, recline		24
ἀνάκειμαι	I lie, recline		14
συνανάκειμαι	I recline with		7
ἀντίκειμαι	I am opposed		8
ἐπίκειμαι	I lie upon, press upon		7
κατάκειμαι	I lie down		12
κοιμάομαι	I sleep, fall asleep, die	(*cem*etery)	18
περίκειμαι	I lie around; I wear		5
πρόκειμαι	I lie before, am present		5

5. κενός, -ή, -όν	empty		18
κενόω	I empty		5

κλάω	I break		14
κλάσμα, -ατος, τό	fragment		9
κλάδος, -ου, ὁ	branch		11

| κλείω | I shut, lock | | 16 |
| κλείς, -δός, ἡ | key | | 6 |

| κλέπτης, -ου, ὁ | thief | (*klept*omaniac) | 16 |
| κλέπτω | I steal | | 13 |

κληρονομέω	I inherit, acquire		18
κληρονομία, -ας, ἡ	inheritance, possession		14
κληρονόμος, -ου, ὁ	heir		15
κλῆρος, -ου, ὁ	lot, share		11

κοινωνία, -ας, ἡ	communion, fellowship, participation		19
κοινωνέω	I share, participate		8
κοινωνός, -οῦ, ὁ and ἡ	companion, partner		10
κοινός, -ή, -όν	communal, common	(*Koine* Greek)	14
κοινόω	I make common, defile		14

κοπιάω	I work		23
κόπος, -ου, ὁ	trouble, work		18
εὐκοπώτερος, -ον	easier		7

| κρύπτω | I hide | (*crypt*) | 19 |
| κρυπτός, -ή, -όν | hidden, secret | | 17 |

| κτίσις, -εως, ἡ | creation, creature | | 19 |
| κτίζω | I create | | 15 |

| λατρεύω | I serve | (cf. ido*later*) | 21 |
| λατρεία, -ας, ἡ | service, worship | | 5 |

| λύχνος, -ου, ὁ | lamp | | 14 |
| λυχνία, -ας, ἡ | lampstand | | 12 |

---

6. | μακροθυμία, -ας, ἡ | patience, steadfastness | | 14 |
μακροθυμέω	I wait patiently		10
μακράν	far away		10
μακρόθεν	from far away		5
μακρός, -ά, -όν	long		14

| μέλει | it is a care | | 10 |
| μεταμέλομαι | I regret, repent | | 6 |

| μεριμνάω | I am anxious; I care for | | 19 |
| μέριμνα, -ης, ἡ | anxiety, care | | 6 |

| μέτρον, -ου, τό | measure | (*metr*ic) | 14 |
| μετρέω | I measure | | 11 |

| μοιχεύω | I commit adultery | | 15 |
| μοιχαλίς, -ίδος, ἡ | adulteress | | 7 |

| μωρός, -ά, -όν | foolish, stupid | (*moron*) | 12 |
| μωρία, -ας, ἡ | foolishness | | 5 |

| νέος, -α, -ον | new, young | (*neo*classical) | 24 |
| νεανίσκος, -ου, ὁ | youth, young man | | 11 |

νηστεύω	I fast		20
νηστεία, -ας, ἡ	fasting		6
νυμφίος, -ου, ὁ	bridegroom		16
νύμφη, -ης, ἡ	bride	(*nymph*)	8
ξένος, -η, -ον	strange, foreign		14
ξενίζω	I entertain; I surprise		10
ξηραίνω	I dry, dry up		15
ξηρός, -ά, -όν	dry	(*xero*graphy)	8
ὅριον, -ου, τό	region		12
ὁρίζω	I determine, appoint	(*horiz*on)	8
προορίζω	I predestine		6
7. παλαιός, -ά, -όν	old	(*paleo*lithic)	19
πάλαι	long ago, for a long time		7
παύω	I cease	(*pau*se)	15
ἀναπαύω	I give rest, refresh		12
ἀνάπαυσις, -εως, ἡ	rest, resting place		5
κατάπαυσις, -εως, ἡ	rest, resting place		9
πενθέω	I grieve, mourn		10
πένθος, -ους, τό	grief, mourning		5
πέραν	across		23
διαπεράω	I cross over		6

πετεινόν, -οῦ, τό	bird		14
πέτομαι	I fly		5
πλεονεξία, -as, ἡ	greediness, covetousness		10
πλεονάζω	I am/become more; I increase		9
πλεονεκτέω	I take advantage, outwit		5
πληγή, -ῆs, ἡ	blow, wound	(*plague*)	22
ἐπιπλήσσω	I strike, reprove		13
ποιμήν, -ένος, ὁ	shepherd		18
ποιμαίνω	I tend, pasture		11
ποίμνη, -ης, ἡ	flock		5
ποίμνιον, -ου, τό	flock		5
πόλεμος, -ου, ὁ	war	(*polem*ics)	18
πολεμέω	I make war		7
πορνεία, -as, ἡ	prostitution, unchastity	(*porn*ography)	25
πορνεύω	I practice prostitution, am sexually immoral		8
πόρνη, -ης, ἡ	prostitute		12
πόρνος, -ου, ὁ	a sexually immoral person		10
8. πυλών, -ῶνος, ὁ	gate, gateway		18
πύλη, -ης, ἡ	gate, door		10
σαλπίζω	I trumpet		12
σάλπιγξ, -ιγγος, ἡ	trumpet		11

| σεισμός, -οῦ, ὁ | shaking, earthquake | (seismic) | 14 |
| σείω | I shake, agitate | | 5 |

σκεῦος, -ους, τό	vessel, jar		23
κατασκευάζω	I prepare, furnish		11
παρασκευή, -ῆς, ἡ	preparation		6

| σκηνή, -ῆς, ἡ | tent, dwelling, tabernacle | (scene) | 20 |
| σκηνόω | I live, dwell | | 5 |

| σπλαγχνίζομαι | I feel sympathy for | | 12 |
| σπλάγχνον, -ου, τό | heart; love, sympathy | | 11 |

9.
σπουδή, -ῆς, ἡ	haste; eagerness		12
σπουδάζω	I hasten; I am eager		11
σπεύδω	I hasten		6

| σφραγίς, -ῖδος, ἡ | seal | | 16 |
| σφραγίζω | I seal | | 15 |

| σχίζω | I split, divide | (schizophrenia) | 11 |
| σχίσμα, -ατος, τό | split, division | (schism) | 8 |

ταπεινόω	I make low, humble		14
ταπεινός, -ή, -όν	lowly, humble		8
ταπεινοφροσύνη, -ης, ἡ	humility		7

ταχέως	quickly		15
τάχος, -ους, τό	speed, quickness		8
ταχύς, -εῖα, -ύ	quick		13

τυγχάνω	I meet, happen	12
ἐντυγχάνω	I appeal to	5
ἐπιτυγχάνω	I obtain, attain to	5

τύπος, -ου, ὁ	image, copy	(*type*)	15
τύπτω	I strike, beat		13

ὑγιαίνω	I am healthy, sound	(cf. *hygiene*)	12
ὑγιής, -ές	healthy, sound		12

10. ὑστερέω	I am in need, fail; (pass.) I lack	16
ὑστέρημα, -ατος, τό	need	9
ὕστερος, -α, -ον	second, later, finally	12

ὑψόω	I lift up	20
ὑψηλός, -ή, -όν	high	11
ὕψιστος, -η, -ον	highest, most exalted	13
ὕψος, -ους, τό	height	6

φονεύω	I murder, kill	12
φόνος, -ου, ὁ	murder, killing	9
φονεύς, -έως, ὁ	murderer	7

χιλιάς, -άδος, ἡ	(a group of) a thousand	23
χίλιοι, -αι, -α	thousands	8

χορτάζω	I feed, fill; (pass.) I eat my fill	16
χόρτος, -ου, ὁ	grass, hay	15

χρυσοῦς, -ῆ, -οῦν	golden	(*chrys*anthemum)	18
χρυσίον, -ου, τό	gold		12
χρυσός, -οῦ, ὁ	gold		10
ψεύδομαι	I lie	(*pseudo*nym)	12
ψεῦδος, -ους, τό	lie		10
ψεύστης, -ου, ὁ	liar		10
ψευδοπροφήτης, -ου, ὁ	false prophet	(*prophet*)	11

III. G. Families With One or More Words
Occurring 5–9 Times

1. ἁγνός, -ή, -όν	pure, holy		8
ἁγνίζω ·	I purify		7
ἀγωνίζομαι	I struggle, fight		8
ἀγών, -ῶνος, ὁ	contest, fight	(cf. *agony*)	6
ἅλας, -ατος, τό	salt	(*hal*ite)	8
ἁλιεύς, -έως, ὁ	fisherman		5
ἀλείφω	I anoint		9
ἐξαλείφω	I wipe away, remove		5
ἀπάτη, -ης, ἡ	deception, deceitfulness		7
ἐξαπατάω	I deceive, cheat		6
βαρέω	I weigh down, burden	(*baro*meter)	6
βάρος, -ους, τό	weight, burden		6
βαρύς, -εῖα, -ύ	heavy		6

βέβαιος, -α, -ον	firm, permanent		8
βεβαιόω	I make firm, establish		8
διαρ(ρ)ήγνυμι or διαρήσσω	I tear, break		7
ῥήγνυμι	I tear, break		5
διασκορπίζω	I scatter, disperse		9
σκορπίος, -ου, ὁ	scorpion	(*scorpion*)	5
διατρίβω	I spend; I stay		9
συντρίβω	I shatter, break		7
ἐνάντιος, -α, -ον	against, opposed, hostile		8
κατέναντι	opposite; before		8
ἀπέναντι	opposite, against		5
ἐπιλανθάνομαι	I forget		8
λανθάνω	I am hidden		6
ἔρις, -ιδος, ἡ	strife, discord		9
ἐριθεία, -ας, ἡ	strife; selfishness		7
2. ζώνη, -ης, ἡ	belt, girdle	(cf. *zone*)	8
περιζώννυμι	I gird about		6
θαρσέω	I am courageous, cheerful		7
θαρρέω	I am confident, courageous		6
κλίνη, -ης, ἡ	bed, couch	(cf. re*cline*)	9
ἀνακλίνω	I cause to lie down; (pass.) I lie down		6

κατακλίνω	I cause to lie down; (pass.) I lie down		5
πρωτοκλισία, -ας, ἡ	the place of honor		5

κόκκος, -ου, ὁ	seed, grain		7
κόκκινος, -η, -ον	red, scarlet		6

κραυγάζω	I cry out, shout		9
κραυγή, -ῆς, ἡ	cry, shout		6

λαμπάς, -άδος, ἡ	torch, lamp	(*lamp*)	9
λαμπρός, -ά, -όν	bright, shining		9
λάμπω	I shine, shine out		7

μαστιγόω	I whip, scourge		7
μάστιξ, -ιγος, ἡ	scourging, torment		6

3. μεθερμηνεύω	I translate	(cf. *hermeneu*tics)	8
διερμηνεύω	I explain, translate		6

μετασχηματίζω	I transform		6
εὐσχήμων, -ον	prominent, of high repute		5

ὀκτώ	eight	(*oct*opus)	6
ὄγδοος, -η, -ον	eighth		5

ὀνειδίζω	I reproach, insult		9
ὀνειδισμός, -οῦ, ὁ	reproach, insult		5

ὀξύς, -εῖα, -ύ	sharp		8
ὄξος, -ους, τό	sour wine, vinegar		6
σκιά, -ᾶς, ἡ	shade, shadow		7
ἐπισκιάζω	I overshadow, cover		5
σκληρύνω	I harden	(multiple *scler*osis)	6
σκληρός, -ά, -όν	hard, difficult		5
στοιχεῖον, -ου, τό	element; heavenly body		7
στοιχέω	I hold to, follow		5
φθείρω	I destroy, ruin		9
φθαρτός, -ή, -όν	perishable, corruptible		6
ἄφθαρτος, -η, -ον	imperishable, incorruptible		8
ἀφθαρσία, -ας, ἡ	incorruptibility, immortality		7
διαφθείρω	I destroy, ruin		6
διαφθορά, -ᾶς, ἡ	destruction, corruption		6
φθορά, -ᾶς, ἡ	destruction		9
χρίω	I anoint	(*chr*isten)	5
ἀντίχριστος, -ου, ὁ	the antichrist[5]	(*antichrist*)	5
ψαλμός, -οῦ, ὁ	song of praise, psalm	(*psalm*)	7
ψάλλω	I sing		5
ᾠδή, -ῆς, ἡ	song	(*ode*)	7
ᾄδω	I sing		5

---

[5] Note that the proper noun Χριστός, "Messiah, Christ," is also a member of this word family.

Part Four

New Testament Greek Vocabulary
without Cognate, Listed by Frequency

IV. A. Words Occurring 400 or More Times

ἀπό	(with gen.) from, away from	(*apo*stasy)	646
γάρ	for		1042
δέ	but, and (frequently untranslated)		2801
διά	(with gen.) through; (with acc.) because of, for the sake of	(*dia*meter)	668
ἐν	(with dat.) in	(cf. *in*)	2757
ἐπί	(with gen.) over, upon; (with dat.) on, in; (with acc.) on, against	(*epi*graph)	891
θεός, -οῦ, ὁ	God, god	(*theo*logy)	1318
οὖν	therefore, then		501

IV. B. Words Occurring 155–399 Times

ἀνήρ, -δρος, ὁ	man	(*andr*oid)	216
γυνή, -αικός, ἡ	woman	(*gyneco*logist)	215
ἔθνος, -ους, τό	nation, the Gentiles	(*ethn*ic)	162
εὑρίσκω	I find, discover	(*heuris*tic)	176
ἤ	or, either		344
εἷς, μία, ἕν[1]	one		346
ὄχλος, -ου, ὁ	multitude		175
παρά	(with gen.) from; (with dat.) at, by; (with acc.) by, near	(*para*site)	194

[1] These three gender-forms of "one" are in reality three separate words, as can readily be seen from their different forms. Each has its own cognates, e.g., οὐδείς, οὐδεμία, οὐδέν, respectively. They are shown together here to aid memorization.

περί	(with gen.) about, concerning; (with acc.) around, near	(*peri*meter)	333
πόλις, -εως, ἡ	city	(*poli*tics)	164
πρῶτος, -η, -ον	first	(*proto*type)	156
τέ	and		215
χείρ, χειρός, ἡ	hand		178

IV. C. Words Occurring 100–154 Times

ἀμήν	so let it be, truly, amen	(*amen*)	130
ἕως	until		146
καρδία, -ας, ἡ	heart	(*cardi*ologist)	151
λαός, -οῦ, ὁ	people	(cf. *lai*ty)	142
μέλλω	I am about to, intend		109
μόνος, -η, -ον	only, alone	(*mono*tone)	115
νεκρός, -ά, -όν	dead	(*necro*logy)	128
ὅλος, -η, -ον	whole, complete	(*holo*gram)	110
πάλιν	again		141
σύν	(with dat.) with	(*syn*tax)	128
σῶμα, -ατος, τό	body	(psycho*soma*tic)	142
ὑπέρ	(with gen.) on behalf of; (with acc.) above	(*hyper*active)	100
ὥρα, -ας, ἡ	hour	(*hor*oscope)	106

IV. D. Words Occurring 50–99 Times

αἷμα, -ατος, τό	blood	(*hem*oglobin)	97
ἀκολουθέω	I follow	(*acolyte*)	90
ἀποκτείνω	I kill		74
ἄρτος, -ου, ὁ	bread		97
γλῶσσα, -ης, ἡ	tongue, language	(*gloss*olalia)	50
εἰρήνη, -ης, ἡ	peace	(*iren*ic)	92
ἕκαστος, -η, -ον	each, every		82
ἔσχατος, -η, -ον	last	(*eschato*logy)	52
ἕτερος, -α, -ον	other, another, different	(*hetero*sexual)	99
ἔτι	yet, still		93
θάλασσα, -ης, ἡ	sea		91
θρόνος, -ου, ὁ	throne	(*throne*)	62

καιρός, -οῦ, ὁ	time, right time		86
κεφαλή, -ῆς, ἡ	head	(en*cephal*itis)	75
μακάριος, -α, -ον	blessed, happy		50
μήτηρ, -τρός, ἡ	mother	(*mater*nal)	83
νύξ, νυκτός, ἡ	night	(cf . *noct*urnal)	61
ὄρος, -ους, τό	mountain, hill		63
πρεσβύτερος,	old; (as a noun) elder	(*Presbyter*ian)	66
-α, -ον			
προσκυνέω	I worship		60
σάββατον,	Sabbath, week	(*Sabbath*)	68
-ου, τό			
στόμα, -ατος, τό	mouth	(*stoma*ch)	78
τόπος, -ου, ὁ	place	(*topo*graphy)	94
τυφλός, -ή, -όν	blind		50
ὕδωρ, -ατος, τό	water	(*hydro*electric)	78

IV. E. Words Occurring 26–49 Times

1. ἅπτω	I kindle; I touch, hold		39
ἄρα	so, then		49
ἀρνίον, -ου, τό	sheep, lamb		30
ἄρτι	now, just		36
ἄχρι	until		49
βαστάζω	I bear		27
γέ	(usually untranslatable particle, emphasizing the word it follows)		28
ἥκω	I have come, am present		26
ἥλιος, -ου, ὁ	sun		32
θεραπεύω	I care for, heal	(*therapeu*tic)	43
θηρίον, -ου, τό	animal		46
θυγάτηρ,	daughter	(cf. *daughter*)	28
-τρός, ἡ			
θύρα, -ας, ἡ	door	(cf. *door*)	39
ἱκανός, -ή, -όν	sufficient, large		39
κελεύω	I command, urge		26
κώμη, -ης, ἡ	village		27

2.

μάχαιρα, -ης, ἡ	sword		29
μέλος, -ους, τό	member, part		34
μικρός, -ά, -όν	small	(*micro*be)	46
μισέω	I hate	(*mis*anthrope)	40
μισθός, -οῦ, ὁ	wages		29
μυστήριον, -ου, τό	mystery, secret rites	(*mystery*)	28
ναί	yes, indeed		33
νικάω	I conquer		28
οἶνος, -ου, ὁ	wine	(cf. *wine*)	34
ὀλίγος, -η, -ον	few, little	(*olig*archy)	41
ὀμνύω/ὄμνυμι	I swear, take an oath		26
οὐαί	woe, alas		47
οὖς, ὠτός, τό	ear		37
πλήν	but, except		31
πτωχός, -ή, -όν	poor		34
χήρα, -ας, ἡ	widow		27

IV. F. Words Occurring 10–25 Times

1.

ἄκανθα, -ης, ἡ	thorn-plant		14
ἀκροβυστία, -ας, ἡ	uncircumcision, the Gentiles		20
ἀλέκτωρ, -ορος, ὁ	cock		12
ἅλυσις, -εως, ἡ	chain		11
ἅμα	together		10
ἀμφότεροι, -αι, -α	both, all		14
ἀντί	(with gen.) in place of, for	(*anti*christ)	22
ἀριθμός, -οῦ, ὁ	number	(*arithm*etic)	18
ἀσέλγεια, -ας, ἡ	licentiousness, sensuality		10
ἀσκός, -οῦ, ὁ	wine-skin		12
αὐξάνω	I grow, increase		23
ἀφορίζω	I separate	(*aphorism*)	10
βροντή, -ῆς, ἡ	thunder	(*bronto*saurus)	12
γέεννα, -ης, ἡ	Gehenna, hell	(*gehenna*)	12

γεύομαι	I taste; I come to know		15
γυμνός, -ή, -όν	naked	(*gymna*sium)	15
δάκρυον -ου, τό	tear		10
δεῖπνον, -ου, τό	dinner, supper		16
δένδρον, -ου, τό	tree	(rhodo*dendron*)	25
δέρω	I beat		15
δεσπότης, -ου, ὁ	lord, master	(*despot*)	10
δηνάριον, -ου, τό	denarius	(*denarius*)	16
δίκτυον, -ου, τό	net		12
διψάω	I thirst		16
δόλος, -ου, ὁ	deceit		11
δράκων, -οντος, ὁ	dragon	(*dragon*)	13
2. ἐάω	I permit; I let go, leave alone		11
ἔθος, -ους, τό	custom, law	(*eth*ic)	12
εἰκών -όνος, ἡ	image	(*icon*)	23
ἐλάχιστος, -ίστη, -ιστον	smallest, least		14
ἐλέγχω	I expose, convict, convince		17
ἔνατος, -η, -ον	ninth		10
ἕνεκεν or ἕνεκα	(with gen.) because of, for the sake of		19
ἐνιαυτός, -οῦ, ὁ	year		14
ἔνοχος, -ον	liable, guilty		10
ἐπίσταμαι	I know, understand		14
θρίξ, τριχός, ἡ	hair		15
ἵππος, -ου, ὁ	horse	(*hippo*potamus)	17
ἰχθύς, -ύος, ὁ	fish		20
κάλαμος, -ου, ὁ	reed		12
καπνός, -οῦ, ὁ	smoke		13
κέρας, -ατος, τό	horn	(trice*ra*tops)	11
κερδαίνω	I gain		17
κοιλία, -ας, ἡ	womb, belly		22
κολλάομαι	I cling to, join		12
κράβαττος, -ου, ὁ	mattress, bed		11

κωλύω	I hinder, forbid		23
κωφός, -ή, -όν	mute, deaf		14
λευκός, -ή, -όν	white	(*leuk*emia)	25
λῃστής, -οῦ, τό	robber		15
λίαν	very (much)		12
λίμνη, -ης, ἡ	lake		11
λιμός, -οῦ, ἡ	hunger, famine		12

3.

μέχρι	until		17
μήν, μηνός, ὁ	month	(*meno*pause)	18
μύρον, -ου, τό	ointment, perfume	(*myrrh*)	14
νεφέλη, -ης, ἡ	cloud		25
νήπιος, -ία, -ιον	infant, minor		15
νίπτω	I wash		17
νόσος, -ου, ἡ	disease, illness		11
ξύλον, -ου, τό	wood, tree; cross	(*xylo*phone)	20
ὀδούς, ὀδόντος, ὁ	tooth	(ortho*dont*ist)	12
ὅρκος, -ου, ὁ	oath		10
ὄφις, -εως, ὁ	snake, serpent		14
παρθένος, -ου, ἡ and ὁ	virgin	(the *Parthen*on)	15
πατάσσω	I strike		10
πεινάω	I hunger		23
περιστερά, -ᾶς, ἡ	pigeon, dove		10
πέτρα, -ας, ἡ	rock, stone	(*Peter*)	15
πηγή, -ῆς, ἡ	spring, fountain		11
πιάζω	I seize, catch		12
πλησίον	near		17
ποικίλος, -η, -ον	manifold		10
ποταμός, -οῦ, ὁ	river, stream	(hippo*potamus*)	17
πραΰτης, -ητος, ἡ	gentleness, humility, meekness		11
πρίν	before		13
προσκαρτερέω	I hold fast to		10
πρωΐ	early (in the morning)		12
πυνθάνομαι	I ask		12

πωλέω	I sell	(mono*poly*)	22
πῶλος, -ου, ἡ	ass's foal, young donkey		12

4. ῥαββί rabbi *(rabbi)* 15

ῥάβδος, -ου, ἡ	rod, staff		12
ῥίζα, -ης, ἡ	root		17
ῥύομαι	I save		17
σαλεύω	I shake		15
σιγάω	I am silent, still		10
σῖτος, -ου, ὁ	wheat, grain		14
σιωπάω	I am silent		10
στέφανος, -ου, ὁ	crown	*(Stephen)*	18
στηρίζω	I establish, strengthen	*(ster*oids)	13
σφάζω	I slaughter		10
σφόδρα	very (much)		11
τάλαντον, -ου, τό	talent	*(talent)*	14
ταράσσω	I trouble		18
τελώνης, -ου, ὁ	tax collector		21
τέρας, -ατος, τό	wonder		16
τολμάω	I dare		16
τράπεζα, -ης, ἡ	table		15
τρέχω	I run	(cf. *trek*)	20
ὑπηρέτης, -ου, ὁ	servant, assistant		20
φείδομαι	I spare		10
φιάλη, -ης, ἡ	bowl	*(vial)*	12
χείρων, -ον	worse		11
χιτών, -ῶνος, ὁ	tunic		11
χοῖρος, -ου, ὁ	swine		12
χωλός, -ή, -όν	lame		14
ὦ	O! Oh!	*(O!)*	17
ὠφελέω	I help		15

IV. G. Words Occurring 5–9 Times

1. ἄβυσσος, -ου, ἡ   abyss, underworld   (*abyss*)   9

ἄβυσσος, -ου, ἡ	abyss, underworld	(*abyss*)	9
ἀγανακτέω	I am indignant		7
ἀγέλη, -ης, ἡ	herd		7
ἀετός, -οῦ, ὁ	eagle		5
ἀήρ, ἀέρος, ὁ	air	(*air*)	7
αἰγιαλός, -οῦ, ὁ	shore		6
ἀκριβῶς	accurately, carefully		9
ἄκρον, -ου, τό	high point, limit	(*acro*phobia)	6
ἄμμος, -ου, ἡ	sand		5
ἄμωμος, -ον	unblemished, blameless		8
ἀνθύπατος, -ου, ὁ	proconsul		5
ἁπλότης, -ητος, ἡ	sincerity		8
ἀποδημέω	I journey		6
ἀποθήκη, -ης, ἡ	storehouse, barn	(*apothe*cary)	6
ἀποστερέω	I steal		6
ἀπωθέομαι	I repudiate		6
ἀργός, -ή, -όν	idle		8
ἀρετή, -ῆς, ἡ	virtue		5
ἀρκέω	I am enough, suffice		8
ἄρρωστος, -ον	sick		5
ἄρσην, -ενος, ὁ	male		9
ἀσύνετος, -ον	foolish	(cf. *asin*ine)	5
ἀσφαλής, -ές	safe, firm		5
ἀφορμή, -ῆς, ἡ	occasion, opportunity		7
βάθος, -ους, τό	depth	(*bath*)	8
βάρβαρος, -ον	strange, foreign	(*barbar*ian)	6
βάτος, -ου, ἡ	thornbush		6
βδέλυγμα, -ατος, τό	abomination		6

2.

βόσκω	I tend, feed		9
βοῦς, -ός, ὁ	ox; (fem.) cow	(cf. *bovine*)	8
βραχύς, -εῖα, -ύ	short, little		7
βρέφος, -ους, τό	baby		8

βρέχω	I send rain		7
βρυγμός, -οῦ, ὁ	gnashing		7
βύσσινος, -η, -ον	made of fine linen		5
γάλα, -ακτος, τό	milk	(*galaxy*)	5
γαστήρ, -τρός, ἡ	belly, womb	(*gastric*)	9
γογγύζω	I murmur		8
δάκτυλος, -ου, ὁ	finger	(ptero*dactyl*)	8
δαπανάω	I spend freely		5
δηλόω	I make clear		7
δίς	twice	(cf. *di-*)	6
δοκός, -οῦ, ἡ	beam		6
δρέπανον, -ου, τό	sickle		8
δῶμα, -ατος, τό	roof, housetop	(*dome*)	7
ἐγκεντρίζω	I graft		6
εἰκῇ	in vain		6
ἐλαύνω	I drive, row		5
ἕλκω	I draw		8
ἐμβριμάομαι	I warn; I am deeply moved		5
ἐμπτύω	I spit on (or) at		6
ἐκμάσσω	I wipe		5
ἐκτείνω	I extend		9
ἐπιεικής, -ές	gentle		6
ἐραυνάω	I search, examine		6
ἐσθής, -ῆτος, ἡ	clothing		8
εὖ	well	(*eu*logy)	6
ἔχιδνα, -ης, ἡ	viper		5
3. ζημιόομαι	I forfeit		6
ζιζάνιον, -ου, τό	weed		8
ζόφος, -ου, ὁ	darkness		5
ζυγός, -οῦ, ὁ	yoke		6
ἡλικία, -ας, ἡ	age, stature		8
ἥμισυς, -εια, -υ	half	(*hemi*sphere)	5
ἡσυχάζω	I am quiet		5
θερμαίνομαι	I warm myself	(cf. *thermo*meter)	6

θόρυβος, -ου, ὁ	noise, turmoil		7
θώραξ, -ακος, ὁ	breastplate	(*thorax*)	5
ἴσος, -η, -ον	equal	(*iso*metrics)	8
κάμηλος, -ου, ὁ	camel	(*camel*)	6
καταπέτασμα, -ατος, τό	curtain		6
κατηχέω	I teach	(*catech*ize)	8
κῆπος, -ου, ὁ	garden		5
κιβωτός, -οῦ, ἡ	ark		6
κίνδυνος, -ου, ὁ	danger		9
κινέω	I move	(*kine*tic)	8
κολαφίζω	I strike		5
κόλπος, -ου, ὁ	breast, chest		6
κονιορτός, -οῦ, ὁ	dust		5
4. κοράσιον, -ου, τό	little girl		8
κόφινος, -ου, ὁ	basket	(*coffin*)	6
κράσπεδον, -ου, τό	hem, tassel		5
κρεμάννυμι	I hang		7
κρούω	I knock		9
κτάομαι	I acquire		7
κύκλῳ	(all) around	(*cycle*)	8
κῦμα, -ατος, τό	wave		5
κύων, -νός, ὁ	dog	(*cyn*ic)	5
λεπρός, -ά, -όν	leprous	(*leper*)	9
λέων, -οντος, ὁ	lion	(*lion*)	9
ληνός, -οῦ, ἡ	wine-press		5
λύκος, -ου, ὁ	wolf		6
μάγος, -ου, ὁ	Magus; magician	(*magic*)	6
μαίνομαι	I am mad	(cf. *man*ia)	5
μαργαρίτης, -ου, ὁ	pearl	(*Margaret*)	9
μάταιος, -αία, -αιον	idle, useless		6
μεθύω	I am drunk	(*methy*l alcohol)	7
μέλας, -αινα, -αν	black	(*melan*choly)	6
μεστός, -ή, -όν	full		9

μιαίνω	I defile		5
μιμητής, -οῦ, ὁ	imitator	(cf. *mime*)	6
μνᾶ, μνᾶς, ἡ	mina		9
μόσχος, -ου, ὁ	calf		6
μῦθος, -ου, ὁ	tale, myth	(*myth*)	5
μυριάς, -άδος, ἡ	ten thousand, myriad	(*myriad*)	8

5.

νῆσος, -ου, ἡ	island		9
νήφω	I am sober, self-controlled		6
νότος, -ου, ὁ	south, south wind		7
ὀθόνιον, -ου, τό	linen cloth		5
οἰκτιρμός, -οῦ, ὁ	mercy		5
ὅπλον, -ου, τό	weapon		6
ὁρμάω	I set out, rush		5
ὅσιος, -ία, -ον	devout, holy		8
ὀσμή, -ῆς, ἡ	odor		6
ὀσφῦς, -ύος, ἡ	waist, loins		8
οὐρά, -ᾶς, ἡ	tail		5
παγίς, -ίδος, ἡ	trap		5
παίω	I strike, wound		5
παρακύπτω	I bend over		5
παροιμία, -ας, ἡ	proverb, figure		5
πενθερά, -ᾶς, ἡ	mother-in-law		6
πεποίθησις, -εως, ἡ	confidence		6
πηλός, -οῦ, ὁ	clay, mud		6
πήρα, -ας, ἡ	bag		6
πίναξ, -ακος, ἡ	dish		5
πιπράσκω	I sell		9
πλατεῖα, -ας, ἡ	street	(*place*)	9
πλευρά, -ᾶς, ἡ	side	(*pleur*isy)	5
πραιτώριον, -ου, τό	praetorium		8
πρέπω	I am fitting		7

6.

πταίω	I stumble		5
πτέρυξ, -υγος, ἡ	wing	(*pter*odactyl)	5

75

πωρόω	I harden		5
ῥίπτω	I throw down		7
ῥομφαία, -ας, ἡ	sword		7
σαπρός, -ά, -όν	rotten		8
σβέννυμι	I extinguish		8
σελήνη, -ης, ἡ	moon		9
σίδηρος, -ου, ὁ	iron		5
σπεῖρα, -ης, ἡ	cohort		7
σπήλαιον, -ου, τό	cave, den	(cf. *spel*unker)	6
σπυρίς, -ίδος, ἡ	basket		5
στάδιον, -ου, τό	stade	(*stadium*)	7
στάχυς, -υος, ὁ	head, ear (of grain)		5
στεῖρα, -ας, ἡ	barren	(cf. *steri*le)	5
στενάζω	I sigh, groan		6
στῆθος, -ους, τό	chest, breast	(*stetho*scope)	5
στρωννύω	I spread		6
συμπνίγω	I crowd out, choke out		5
σύρω	I draw		5
τεῖχος, -ους, τό	(city) wall		9
τράχηλος, -ου, τό	neck, throat	(*trache*a)	7
τρόμος, -ου, ὁ	trembling	(*tremo*r)	5
τρώγω	I eat (audibly)		6
7. ὑβρίζω	I treat arrogantly, insult	(cf. *hubris*)	5
ὑετός, -οῦ, ὁ	rain	(cf. *wet*)	5
ὑπερήφανος, -ον	arrogant, haughty		5
ὕπνος, -ου, ὁ	sleep	(*hypno*tism)	6
φαῦλος, -η, -ον	worthless, evil		6
φθάνω	I arrive; I precede		7
φθόνος, -ου, ὁ	envy		9
φλόξ, φλογός, ἡ	flame		7
φρέαρ, -ατος, τό	a well		7
φύλλον, -ου, τό	leaf	(chloro*phyll*)	6
φύραμα, -ατος, τό	dough		5
φυσιόω	I puff up, make proud		7
χαλκός, -οῦ, ὁ	brass, bronze, money		5

χάραγμα, -ατος, τό	mark, stamp	(cf. *charac*ter)	8
χεῖλος, -ους, τό	lip		7
χειμών, -ῶνος, ὁ	winter, stormy weather		6
ὡσαννά	hosanna!		6

Part Five

Helps for Verb Analysis

An important, and probably the most challenging, part of learning the vocabulary of the Greek New Testament is learning the principal parts of numerous verbs. The student often learns these one by one in the daily lessons, but it is good to review them together. This section presents helps for learning and understanding the structure of verbs. First is a chart on the principal parts, tense systems, and aspects of the regular verb; second is an explanation of the elements of verb structure, especially as they are used in parsing verbs; and third is a list of the principal parts of many important verbs, arranged by type.

A. Principal Parts, Tense Systems, and Aspects of the Regular Verb

λύω   1. PRESENT SYSTEM

       a. *Present tense* (active, middle, passive)   All moods

          Stem + ending (λυ-ομεν)

          Indicative – continuing action in the present time

          Other forms – continuing action, time undetermined

       b. *Imperfect tense* (active, middle, passive)

          Augment + stem + ending (ἐ-λυ-ομεν)

          In the indicative mood *only* (continued action in past)

λύσω   2. FUTURE SYSTEM

       Future tense (active & mid.) No subjunctive or imperative

       Stem + σ + ending (λυ-σ-ομεν)

       Continued action in future

ἔλυσα   3. FIRST AORIST SYSTEM

       1st Aorist Tense (active & middle)   All moods

       (Augment) + stem + σ + a-type ending (ἐ-λυ-σ-αμεν)

       Indicative (with augment) – undefined action in past

       Other moods (no augment) – undefined action, time undetermined

78

λέλυκα   4. FIRST PERFECT ACTIVE SYSTEM

        a. *Perfect tense* (active only)   All moods

           Reduplication + stem + κ + a-type ending

           (λε-λυ-κ-αμεν)

           Indicative – completed action in present

           Other moods – completed action

        b. *Pluperfect tense* (active only)

           Augment + reduplication + stem + κ + ending

           (ἐ-λε-λυ-κ-εμεν)

           In the indicative mood *only* (completed action in the past)

λέλυμαι   5. PERFECT MIDDLE AND PASSIVE SYSTEM

        a. *Perfect tense* (middle and passive)   All moods

           Reduplication + stem + middle-passive ending

           (λε-λυ-μεθα)

           Indicative – completed action in present

           Other moods – completed action

        b. *Pluperfect tense* (middle and passive)

           Augment + reduplication + stem + mid.-pass. ending

           (ἐ-λε-λυ-μεθα)

           In the indicative mood *only* (completed action in the past)

ἐλύθην   6. FIRST PASSIVE SYSTEM

        a. *Aorist tense* (passive only)   All moods

           (Augment) + stem + $\theta\eta$ + active ending   (ἐ-λυ-θη-μεν)

           Indicative (with augment) – undefined action in past

           Other moods (no augment) – undefined action, time unde-

           termined

        b. *Future tense* (passive only)   No subjunctive or imperative

           Stem + $\theta\eta$ + σ + passive ending   (λυ-θη-σ-ομεθα)

           Continued action in the future

B. Elements of Verb Structure for Parsing

Students are often called upon to "parse" (analyze grammatically) verbs of all sorts. Here is an explanation of verb structure necessary for parsing efficiently; it should be used for consolidation and review.

All verbs have some or all of the following elements:

1. **Tense**: Present, Imperfect, Future, Aorist, Perfect, Pluperfect, Future Perfect (rare)

2. **Aspect**: Continual, Undetermined, Perfective

3. **Voice**: Active, Middle, Passive

4. **Mood**: Indicative, Subjunctive, Optative, Imperative, Infinitive, Participle (Some grammarians do not consider the infinitive and participle to be moods, but we will consider them so here for pedagogical reasons.)

5. **Person**: First, Second, Third

6. **Number**: Singular, Plural

All tenses occur in all voices, persons, and numbers, but some of the tenses occur in only a limited group of moods:

1. Present tense: all moods

2. Imperfect tense: Indicative mood only

3. Future tense: Indicative, Optative, Infinitive, and Participle

4. Aorist tense: all moods

5. Perfect tense: all moods

6. Pluperfect tense: Indicative mood only

7. Future perfect tense: Indicative, Optative, Infinitive, and Participle (This tense is seldom used, and then almost always in the passive voice.)

Aspects of verbs are directly related to tense:

1. Continual aspect: Present, Imperfect and Future tenses

2. Undetermined aspect: Aorist tense only

3. Perfective aspect: Perfect and Pluperfect tenses

80

In order to parse and translate a verb correctly the student must be able to give the following information:

For **Finite Verbs** (i.e., indicative, subjunctive, optative, imperative): tense, aspect, voice, mood, person and number. Here, for example, is the parsing of λύω:

Tense	Aspect	Voice	Mood	Person	Number
Present	Continual	Active	Indicative	First	Singular

For **Infinitives:** tense, aspect, voice and "mood." Here, for example, is λύειν:

Tense	Aspect	Voice	"Mood"
Present	Continual	Active	Infinitive

For **Participles:** tense, aspect, voice, "mood," gender, number and case. Here, for example, is λύων:

Tense	Aspect	Voice	"Mood"	Gender	Number	Case
Present	Continual	Active	Participle	Masculine	Singular	Nominative

C. Principal Parts of Common Verbs, Arranged by Type

The Greek verb forms its principal parts in rather regular ways. Students who master these patterns will have come a good distance in learning to read rapidly, and understand, the New Testament. The following sections contain all the verbs in the New Testament that occur fifty or more times; they represent fully all the different types of verbs. Where no form appears, that principal part does not occur in the New Testament. Hyphenated forms are found only in compounds.

81

1. Omega-type verbs

Omega-type verbs are by far the most common type. Below are listed both active and middle forms occurring fifty times or more. Although it does not occur more than fifty times in the New Testament apart from compounds, λύω is given first as paradigmatic.

Present	Future	Aorist	Perfect Active	Perfect Middle	Aorist Passive	Meaning
λύω	λύσω	ἔλυσα	λέλυκα	λέλυμαι	ἐλύθην	loose
ἄγω	ἄξω	ἤγαγον		-ῆγμαι	ἤχθην	lead
ἀκούω	ἀκούσω	ἤκουσα	ἀκήκοα		ἠκούσθην	listen
ἀνοίγω	ἀνοίξω	ἀνέῳξα	ἀνέῳγα	ἀνέῳγμαι	ἀνεῴχθην	open
ἄρχω	ἄρξω	ἦρξα				rule
ἀσπάζομαι		ἠσπασάμην				salute
βαπτίζω	βαπτίσω	ἐβάπτισα		βεβάπτισμαι	ἐβαπτίσθην	baptize
βλέπω	βλέψω	ἔβλεψα				see
γίνομαι	γενήσομαι	ἐγενόμην	γέγονα	γεγένημαι	ἐγενήθην	become
γινώσκω	γνώσομαι	ἔγνων	ἔγνωκα	ἔγνωσμαι	ἐγνώσθην	know
γράφω	γράψω	ἔγραψα	γέγραφα	γέγραμμαι	ἐγράφην	write
δέχομαι		ἐδεξάμην		δέδεγμαι	ἐδέχθην	receive
διδάσκω	διδάξω	ἐδίδαξα			ἐδιδάχθην	teach
δοξάζω	δοξάσω	ἐδόξασα		δεδόξασμαι	ἐδοξάσθην	glorify
δύναμαι	δυνήσομαι				ἐδυνήθην	be able
εὐαγγελίζω		εὐηγγέλισα		εὐηγγέλισμαι	εὐηγγελίσθην	preach good news

κηρύσσω	κηρύξω	ἐκήρυξα		κεκήρυγμαι	ἐκηρύχθην	proclaim
κράζω	κράξω	ἔκραξα	κέκραγα			shout
πέμπω	πέμψω	ἔπεμψα			ἐπέμφθην	send
πιστεύω	πιστεύσω	ἐπίστευσα	πεπίστευκα	πεπίστευμαι	ἐπιστεύθην	believe
πορεύομαι	πορεύσομαι			πεπόρευμαι	ἐπορεύθην	proceed
προσεύχομαι	προσεύξομαι	προσηυξάμην				worship
σῴζω	σώσω	ἔσωσα	σέσωκα	σέσωσμαι	ἐσώθην	save
φέρω	οἴσω	ἤνεγκα	-ενήνοχα		ἠνέχθην	bring
χαίρω	χαρήσομαι				ἐχάρην	rejoice

2. Contract verbs
A. Epsilon contracts

αἰτέω	αἰτήσω	ᾔτησα	ᾔτηκα		ᾐτήθην	ask
δοκέω	δόξω	ἔδοξα				seem
ζητέω	ζητήσω	ἐζήτησα			ἐζητήθην	seek
καλέω	καλέσω	ἐκάλεσα	κέκληκα	κέκλημαι	ἐκλήθην	call
λαλέω	λαλήσω	ἐλάλησα	λελάληκα	λελάλημαι	ἐλαλήθην	speak
μαρτυρέω	μαρτυρήσω	ἐμαρτύρησα	μεμαρτύρηκα	μεμαρτύρημαι	ἐμαρτυρήθην	witness
περιπατέω	περιπατήσω	περιεπάτησα				walk
ποιέω	ποιήσω	ἐποίησα	πεποίηκα	πεποίημαι		do, make
τηρέω	τηρήσω	ἐτήρησα	τετήρηκα	τετήρημαι	ἐτηρήθην	keep
φοβέομαι	φοβήσομαι				ἐφοβήθην	fear

83

B. Alpha contracts

ἀγαπάω	ἀγαπήσω	ἠγάπησα	ἠγάπηκα	ἠγάπημαι	ἠγαπήθην	love
γεννάω	γεννήσω	ἐγέννησα	γεγέννηκα	γεγέννημαι	ἐγεννήθην	beget

C. Omicron contracts

πληρόω	πληρώσω	ἐπλήρωσα	πεπλήρωκα	πεπλήρομαι	ἐπληρώθην	fill, fulfill

3. Liquid verbs

αἴρω	ἀρῶ	ἦρα	ἦρκα	ἦρμαι	ἤρθην	take up
ἀποστέλλω	ἀποστελῶ	ἀπέστειλα	ἀπέσταλκα	ἀπέσταλμαι	ἀπεστάλην	send
ἐγείρω	ἐγερῶ	ἤγειρα		ἐγήγερμαι	ἠγέρθην	raise
θέλω		ἠθέλησα				will
κρίνω	κρινῶ	ἔκρινα	κέκρικα	κέκριμαι	ἐκρίθην	judge
μένω	μενῶ	ἔμεινα	μεμένηκα			remain
σπείρω	σπερῶ	ἔσπειρα		ἔσπαρμαι	ἐσπάρην	sow

4. Second Aorists

ἀποθνῄσκω	ἀποθανοῦμαι	ἀπέθανον	τέθνηκα			die
βάλλω	βαλῶ	ἔβαλον	βέβληκα	βέβλημαι	ἐβλήθην	throw
ἔρχομαι	ἐλεύσομαι	ἦλθον	ἐλήλυθα			come
ἐσθίω	φάγομαι	ἔφαγον				eat
ἔχω	ἕξω	ἔσχον	ἔσχηκα			have
λαμβάνω	λήμψομαι	ἔλαβον	εἴληφα			take

84

λέγω	ἐρῶ	εἶπον	εἴρηκα	εἴρημαι	ἐρρέθην	say
ὁράω	ὄψομαι	εἶδον	ἑώρακα		ὤφθην	see
πίνω	πίομαι	ἔπιον	πέπωκα	-πέπτωμαι	-επόθην	drink
πίπτω	πεσοῦμαι	ἔπεσον	πέπτωκα			fall

5. MI-verbs

ἀπόλλυμι	ἀπολέσω	ἀπώλεσα	ἀπόλωλα			destroy
ἀφίημι	ἀφήσω	ἀφῆκα	ἀφεῖκα	ἀφεῖμαι	ἀφέθην	forgive
δίδωμι	δώσω	ἔδωκα	δέδωκα	δέδομαι	ἐδόθην	give
ἵστημι	στήσω	ἔστησα	ἔστηκα		ἐστάθην	stand
τίθημι	θήσω	ἔθηκα	τέθεικα	τέθειμαι	ἐτέθην	place
φημί						say

[a defective verb; the only other form that occurs in other principal parts is ἔφη, the third singular of both the imperfect and the second aorist]

Part Six

Prepositions

A. Proper Prepositions

ἀνά	(with acc.) up;	
	(with numbers) each, apiece	
ἀντί	(with gen.) in place of, for	(*anti*christ)
ἀπό	(with gen.) from, away from	(*apo*stasy)
διά	(with gen.) through;	(*dia*meter)
	(with acc.) because of, for the sake of	
εἰς	(with acc.) into, in	(*eis*egesis)
ἐκ	(with gen.) from, out of	(*ex*hale)
ἐν	(with dat.) in	(*in*)
ἐπί	(with gen.) over, upon;	(*epi*graph)
	(with dat.) on, in;	
	(with acc.) on, against	
κατά	(with gen.) down, against	(*cata*lytic)
	(with acc.) according to, along	
μετά	(with gen.) with;	
	(with acc.) after, behind	(*meta*physics)
παρά	(with gen.) from;	
	(with dat.) at, by;	(*para*medic)
	(with acc.) by, near	
περί	(with gen.) about, concerning;	(*peri*meter)
	(with acc.) around, near	
πρό	(with gen.) before, in front of	(*pro*logue)
πρός	(with dat.) near, at;	(*pros*thetic)
	(with acc.) to, toward	
σύν	(with dat.) with	(*syn*thesis)
ὑπέρ	(with gen.) on behalf of;	
	(with acc.) above	(*hyper*active)
ὑπό	(with gen.) by;	
	(with acc.) under	(*hypo*dermic)

B. Improper Prepositions

ἅμα	together	
ἄνω	above, upward	
ἀπέναντι	opposite, against	
ἐγγύς	near	
ἔμπροσθεν	in front of, before	
ἕνεκεν, ἕνεκα	because of, for the sake of	
ἐνώπιον	before	
ἐκτός	outside	(*ecto*plasm)
ἔξω	outside, out	
ἔξωθεν	from outside	
ἐπάνω	above, over	
ἔσω	in, inside	(*eso*teric)
ἔσωθεν	inside, within; from within	
ἕως	until	
κύκλῳ	(all) around	(*cycle*)
μέσος	middle, in the middle	(*Meso*potamia)
μεταξύ	between	
μέχρι	until	
ὄπισθεν	from behind	
ὀπίσω	behind, back	
πέραν	across	
πλήν	except	
πλησίον	near	
ὑποκάτω	under	
χάριν	for the sake of	
χωρίς	without, apart from	

Part Seven

Conjunctions, Negatives and Adverbs

A special challenge to the student of Greek is often posed by particles, small words that are indeclinable, often compounded, and frequently similar to each other in Greek spelling and English meaning. Few, if any, have English derivatives. These words are important in reading and interpreting, and a little extra study to learn them carefully will pay good dividends. Most particles are conjunctions, negatives, or adverbs; these important particles from Parts Three and Four are presented again here for review.

Conjunctions

ἀλλά	but (strong adversative)
δέ	and, but (mild adversative; postpositive [does not stand first in its clause])
ἄν	(usually untranslatable, but with a generally conditional meaning such as "should, could")
ἄρα	so, then (postpositive)
γάρ	for (postpositive)
γέ	indeed, even (postpositive)
ἐάν	if (takes a verb in the subjunctive mood)
εἰ	if
ἵνα	in order that, that (takes a verb in the subjunctive)
καί	and, also, likewise (καί . . . καί, "both . . . and")
ὅτι	that, because, since
οὖν	therefore
ὥστε	therefore, so that

Negatives

οὐ	no, not (used with indicative verbs; emphatic form is οὐχί)
οὐδέ	and not, nor (οὐδέ . . . οὐδέ, "neither . . . nor"; all forms are used with indicative verbs)
μή	no, not (used with non-indicative verbs)
μηδέ	and not, nor yet (μηδέ . . . μηδέ, "neither . . . nor"; all forms are used with non-indicative verbs)

88

Adverbs

ἄνωθεν	again, from above
εὐθέως	immediately
ἤδη	now, already
μάκροθεν	from afar
μηκέτι	no longer (used with non-indicative verbs)
ὅτε	when
οὐδέποτε	never
οὐκέτι	no more, no longer (used with indicative verbs)
οὔπω	not yet
ποῦ	where? (note that this and the next three adverbs beginning with π are interrogatives)
πόθεν	from where?
πότε	when?
πῶς	how?
σήμερον	today
τότε	then
πάντοτε	always

Part Eight

Numbers

The following numbers and related words from Parts Three and Four are brought together here for greater ease in memorization and review.

———

εἷς, μία, ἕν one

———

δύο two   (*du*et)
δεύτερος, -α, -ον second   (*Deuter*onomy)

———

τρεῖς, τρία three   (cf. *tri*nity)
τρίς three times
τρίτος, -η, -ον third
τριάκοντα thirty

———

τέσσαρες four
τεσσαράκοντα forty
τέταρτος, -η, -ον fourth
τετρακισχίλιοι four thousand
εἰκοσιτέσσαρες twenty-four

———

πέντε five   (*penta*gon)
πεντήκοντα fifty
πεντακισχίλιοι five thousand

———

ἕξ six
ἕκτος, -η, -ον sixth
ἑξήκοντα sixty

———

ἑπτά seven
ἕβδομος, -η, -ον seventh

ὀκτώ eight   (*octo*pus)
ὄγδοος, -η, -ον eighth

δέκα ten   (*deca*de)

δώδεκα twelve

δεκατέσσαρες fourteen

χιλιάς, -άδος, ἡ (a group of) a thousand
χίλιοι, -αι, -α thousands

Index to Parts Three and Four

ἀρχιερεύς 26

ἄρχω 33

ἄρχων 33

ἀσέβεια 53

ἀσεβής 53

ἀσέλγεια 68

ἀσθένεια 41

ἀσθενέω 41

ἀσθενής 41

ἀσκός 68

ἀσπάζομαι 33

ἀσπασμός 33

ἀστήρ 51

ἀστραπή 51

ἀσύνετος 72

ἀσφαλής 72

ἀτιμάζω 48

ἀτιμία 48

αὐξάνω 68

αὔριον 52

αὐτός 12

ἀφαιρέω 50

ἀφανίζω 48

ἄφεσις 26

ἀφθαρσία 64

ἄφθαρτος 64

ἀφίημι 26

ἀφίστημι 28

ἀφορίζω 68

ἀφορμή 72

ἄφρων 49

ἄχρι 67

Β

βάθος 72

βάλλω 26

βαπτίζω 33

βάπτισμα 33

βαπτιστής 33

βάρβαρος 72

βαρέω 61

βάρος 61

βαρύς 61

βασανίζω 51

βασανισμός 51

βαστάζω 67

βασιλεία 20

βασιλεύς 20

βασιλεύω 20

βασιλικός 20

βάτος 72

βδέλυγμα 72

βέβαιος 62

βεβαιόω 62

βιβλίον 41

βίβλος 41

βλασφημέω 30

βλασφημία 30

βλέπω 26

βοάω 51

βοηθέω 51

βόσκω 72

βουλεύομαι 41

βουλή 41

βούλομαι 41

βοῦς 72

βραχύς 72

βρέφος 72

βρέχω 73

βροντή 68

βρυγμός 73

βρῶμα 51

βρῶσις 51

βύσσινος 73

Γ

γαζοφυλακεῖον 49

γάλα 73

γαμέω 41

γαμίζω 41

γάμος 41

γαστήρ 73

γάρ 65

γέ 67

γέεννα 69

γεμίζω 51

γέμω 51

γενεά 13

γένεσις 13

γεννάω 13

γένος 13

γεύομαι 69

γεωργός 20

γῆ 20

γίνομαι 13

γινώσκω 20

γλῶσσα 66

γνώμη 20

γνωρίζω 20

γνῶσις 20

γνωστός 20

γογγύζω 73

γονεῖς 13

γόνυ 52

γράμμα 20

γραμματεύς 20

γραφή 20

γράφω 20

γρηγορέω 27

γυμνός 69

γυνή 65

γωνία 52

ἐγκακέω 35
ἐγκαλέω 28
ἐγκαταλείπω 36
ἐγκεντρίζω 73
ἐγκόπτω 52
ἐγώ 13
ἔθνος 65
ἔθος 69
εἰ 13
εἰδωλόθυτος 23
εἰδωλολάτρης 23
εἴδωλον 23
εἰκῇ 73
εἰκοσιτέσσαρες 47
εἰκών 69
εἰμί 13
εἰρήνη 66
εἰς 14
εἷς 65
εἰσάγω 32
εἰσακούω 12
εἰσέρχομαι 14
εἴσοδος 29
εἰσπορεύομαι 30
εἰσφέρω 39
εἶτα 53
ἐκ 14
ἕκαστος 66
ἑκατοντάρχης 33
ἐκβάλλω 26
ἐκδέχομαι 33
ἐκδικέω 34
ἐκδίκησις 34
ἐκδύω 42
ἐκεῖ 21
ἐκεῖθεν 21

ἐκεῖνος 21
ἐκζητέω 27
ἐκκλησία 28
ἐκκόπτω 52
ἐκλέγομαι 16
ἐκλεκτός 16
ἐκλογή 16
ἐκλύομαι 36
ἐκμάσσω 73
ἐκπίπτω 37
ἐκπορεύομαι 30
ἔκστασις 28
ἐκτείνω 73
ἐκτός 14
ἔκτος 52
ἐκτρέπομαι 53
ἐκφέρω 39
ἐκφεύγω 48
ἐλαία 52
ἔλαιον 52
ἐλαύνω 73
ἐλάχιστος 69
ἐλέγχω 69
ἐλεέω 42
ἐλεημοσύνη 42
ἔλεος 42
ἕλκω 73
ἐλπίζω 34
ἐλπίς 34
ἐμαυτοῦ 13
ἐμβλέπω 26
ἐμβριμάομαι 73
ἐμός 13
ἐμπαίζω 37
ἐμπίμπλημι 38
ἐμπίπτω 37

ἔμπορος 30
ἔμπροσθεν 18
ἐμπτύω 73
ἐμφανίζω 48
ἔμφοβος 40
ἐν 65
ἐνάντιος 62
ἔνατος 69
ἐνδείκνυμι 41
ἔνδυμα 42
ἐνδυναμόω 21
ἐνδύω 42
ἕνεκα 69
ἕνεκεν 69
ἐνεργέω 21
ἐνέργεια 21
ἐνθάδε 52
ἔνι 14
ἐνιαυτός 69
ἐνίστημι 28
ἐνοικέω 29
ἔνοχος 69
ἐντέλλομαι 34
ἐντεῦθεν 52
ἔντιμος 48
ἐντολή 34
ἐντρέπω 53
ἐντυγχάνω 60
ἐνώπιον 30
ἐξ 14
ἕξ 52
ἐξάγω 32
ἐξαιρέω 50
ἐξαλείφω 61
ἐξαπατάω 61
ἐξαυτῆς 12

Z
ζάω 27
ζῆλος 53
ζηλόω 53
ζηλωτής 53
ζημιόομαι 73
ζητέω 27
ζήτημα 27
ζήτησις 27
ζιζάνιον 73
ζόφος 73
ζυγός 73
ζύμη 53
ζωή 27
ζώνη 62
ζῷον 27
ζῳοποιέω 18

Η
ἤ 65
ἡγεμών 43
ἡγέομαι 43
ἤδη 35
ἥκω 67
ἡλικία 73
ἥλιος 67
ἡμέρα 22
ἡμέτερος 13
ἥμισυς 73
ἡσυχάζω 73

Θ
θάλασσα 66
θάνατος 27
θανατόω 27
θαρρέω 62
θαρσέω 62

θαυμάζω 43
θαυμαστός 43
θεάομαι 35
θέλημα 22
θέλω 22
θεμέλιον 53
θεμέλιος 53
θεμελιόω 53
θεός 65
θεραπεύω 67
θερίζω 54
θερισμός 54
θερμαίνομαι 73
θεωρέω 35
θηρίον 67
θησαυρίζω 54
θησαυρός 54
θλίβω 43
θλῖψις 43
θνήσκω 27
θνητός 27
θόρυβος 74
θρίξ 69
θρόνος 66
θυγάτηρ 67
θυμίαμα 43
θυμός 42
θύρα 67
θυσία 43
θυσιαστήριον 43
θύω 43
θώραξ 74

Ι
ἰάομαι 44
ἰατρός 44
ἴδε 23

ἴδιος 28
ἰδιώτης 28
ἰδού 23
ἱερεύς 26
ἱερόν 26
ἱκανός 67
ἱμάτιον 35
ἱματισμός 35
ἵνα 15
ἱνατί 15
ἵππος 69
ἵστημι 28
ἴσος 74
ἰσχυρός 44
ἰσχύς 44
ἰσχύω 44
ἰχθύς 69

Κ
κἀγώ 15
καθαιρέω 50
καθαρίζω 40
καθαρισμός 40
καθαρός 40
καθότι 18
καί 15
καίπερ 15
καιρός 67
καίω 54
κἀκεῖ 15
κἀκεῖθεν 15
κἀκεῖνος 15
κακία 35
κακός 35
κακόω 35
κακῶς 35
κάλαμος 69

κρούω 74
κρυπτός 55
κρύπτω 55
κτάομαι 74
κτίζω 55
κτίσις 55
κύκλῳ 74
κῦμα 74
κυριεύω 15
κύριος 15
κύων 74
κωλύω 70
κώμη 67
κωφός 70

Λ

λαλέω 22
λαμβάνω 22
λαμπάς 63
λαμπρός 63
λάμπω 63
λανθάνω 62
λαός 66
λατρεία 56
λατρεύω 56
λέγω 15
λείπω 36
λειτουργία 21
λειτουργός 22
λεπρός 74
λευκός 70
λέων 74
ληνός 74
λῃστής 70
λίαν 70
λιθάζω 36
λιθοβολέω 26

λίθος 36
λίμνη 70
λιμός 70
λογίζομαι 15
λόγος 15
λοιπός 36
λύκος 74
λυπέω 44
λύπη 44
λυχνία 56
λύχνος 56
λύω 36

Μ

μάγος 74
μαθητής 23
μαίνομαι 74
μακάριος 67
μακράν 56
μακρόθεν 56
μακροθυμέω 56
μακροθυμία 56
μακρός 56
μάλιστα 36
μᾶλλον 36
μανθάνω 23
μαργαρίτης 74
μαρτυρέω 36
μαρτυρία 36
μαρτύριον 36
μαρτύρομαι 36
μάρτυς 36
μαστιγόω 63
μάστιξ 63
μάταιος 74
μάχαιρα 68
μεγαλύνω 23

μέγας 23
μεθερμηνεύω 63
μεθίστημι 28
μεθύω 74
μέλας 74
μέλει 56
μέλλω 66
μέλος 68
μέν 23
μέντοι 23
μένω 29
μερίζω 44
μέριμνα 56
μεριμνάω 56
μερίς 44
μέρος 44
μεσίτης 37
μέσος 37
μεστός 74
μετά 16
μεταδίδωμι 13
μεταλαμβάνω 22
μεταμέλομαι 56
μετανοέω 44
μετάνοια 44
μεταξύ 16
μεταπέμπομαι 37
μετασχηματίζω 63
μετέχω 15
μέτοχος 15
μετρέω 56
μέτρον 56
μέτωπον 30
μέχρι 70
μή 16
μηδέ 16

ὅραμα 16
ὁράω 16
ὀργή 45
ὀργίζομαι 45
ὁρίζω 57
ὅριον 57
ὅρκος 70
ὁρμάω 75
ὅρος 67
ὅς 17
ὅσιος 75
ὀσμή 75
ὅσος 17
ὅστις 17
ὀσφῦς 75
ὅταν 19
ὅτε 17
ὅτι 17
οὐ 17
οὖ 17
οὐαί 68
οὐδέ 17
οὐδείς 17
οὐδέποτε 17
οὐκέτι 17
οὖν 65
οὔπω 17
οὐρά 75
οὐράνιος 24
οὐρανός 24
οὖς 68
οὔτε 17
οὗτος 17
οὕτως 17
οὐχί 17
ὀφειλέτης 45

ὀφείλω 45
ὀφθαλμός 30
ὄφις 70
ὄχλος 65

Π

παγίς 75
πάθημα 45
παιδεία 37
παιδεύω 37
παιδίον 37
παιδίσκη 37
παῖς 37
παίω 75
πάλαι 57
παλαιός 57
πάλιν 66
πανουργία 22
πανταχοῦ 17
παντοκράτωρ 17
πάντοτε 24
πάντως 17
παρά 65
παραβολή 26
παραγγελία 19
παραγγέλλω 19
παραγίνομαι 13
παράγω 32
παραδέχομαι 33
παραδίδωμι 13
παράδοσις 13
παραιτέομαι 32
παρακαλέω 29
παράκλησις 29
παράκλητος 29
παρακύπτω 75
παραλαμβάνω 22

παραλύομαι 36
παραλυτικός 36
παραπορεύομαι 30
παράπτωμα 37
παρασκευή 59
παρατηρέω 39
παρατίθημι 31
παραχρῆμα 49
πάρειμι 14
παρεμβολή 26
παρέρχομαι 14
παρέχω 15
παρθένος 70
παρίστημι 28
παροιμία 75
παρουσία 14
παρρησία 38
παρρησιάζομαι 38
πᾶς 17
πάσχω 45
πατάσσω 70
πατέω 37
πατήρ 17
πατρίς 17
παύω 57
πείθω 24
πεινάω 70
πειράζω 45
πειρασμός 45
πέμπω 37
πενθερά 75
πενθέω 57
πένθος 57
πεντακισχίλιοι 46
πέντε 46
πεντήκοντα 46

προλέγω 16
προορίζω 57
προπέμπω 37
πρός 18
προσάγω 32
προσδέχομαι 33
προσδοκάω 33
προσέρχομαι 14
προσευχή 38
προσεύχομαι 38
προσέχω 15
προσκαλέομαι 29
προσκαρτερέω 70
πρόσκομμα 52
προσκόπτω 52
προσκυνέω 67
προσλαμβάνομαι 22
προσμένω 29
προσπίπτω 37
προστάσσω 48
προστίθημι 31
προσφέρω 39
προσφορά 39
προσφωνέω 31
πρόσωπον 30
πρότερος 46
πρόφασις 30
προφητεία 30
προφητεύω 30
προφήτης 30
πρωΐ 71
πρωτοκλισία 63
πρῶτος 66
πρωτότοκος 39
πταίω 75
πτέρυξ 75

πτῶμα 37
πτωχός 68
πύλη 58
πυλών 58
πυνθάνομαι 71
πῦρ 38
πυρετός 38
πυρόομαι 38
πωλέω 71
πῶλος 71
πώποτε 31
πωρόω 76
πώς 30
πῶς 30

Ρ
ραββί 71
ῥάβδος 71
ῥήγνυμι 62
ῥῆμα 38
ῥίζα 71
ῥίπτω 76
ρομφαία 76
ῥύομαι 71

Σ
σάββατον 67
σαλεύω 71
σάλπιγξ 58
σαλπίζω 58
σαπρός 76
σαρκικός 31
σάρξ 31
σβέννυμι 76
σεαυτοῦ 18
σέβομαι 53
σεισμός 59

σείω 59
σελήνη 76
σημαίνω 39
σημεῖον 39
σήμερον 22
σιγάω 71
σίδηρος 76
σῖτος 71
σιωπάω 71
σκανδαλίζω 47
σκάνδαλον 47
σκεῦος 59
σκηνή 59
σκηνόω 59
σκιά 64
σκληρός 64
σκληρύνω 64
σκοπέω 53
σκορπίος 62
σκοτία 47
σκοτίζομαι 47
σκότος 47
σός 18
σοφία 39
σοφός 39
σπεῖρα 76
σπείρω 39
σπέρμα 39
σπεύδω 59
σπήλαιον 76
σπλαγχνίζομαι 59
σπλάγχνον 59
σπόρος 39
σπουδάζω 59
σπουδή 59
σπυρίς 76

τρίτος 39
τρόμος 76
τρόπος 53
τρώγω 76
τυγχάνω 60
τύπος 60
τύπτω 60
τυφλός 67

Υ

ὑβρίζω 76
ὑγιαίνω 60
ὑγιής 60
ὕδωρ 67
ὑετός 76
υἱοθεσία 24
υἱός 24
ὑμέτερος 18
ὑπάγω 32
ὑπακοή 12
ὑπακούω 12
ὑπάρχω 33
ὑπέρ 66
ὑπερβάλλω 26
ὑπερβολή 26
ὑπερέχω 15
ὑπερήφανος 76
ὑπηρέτης 71
ὕπνος 76
ὑπό 25
ὑπόδειγμα 42
ὑποδείκνυμι 42
ὑπόδημα 41
ὑποκάτω 25
ὑπόκρισις 20
ὑποκριτής 20
ὑπολαμβάνω 22

ὑπομένω 29
ὑπομιμνήσκω 45
ὑπομονή 29
ὑποπόδιον 38
ὑπόστασις 28
ὑποστρέφω 43
ὑποτάσσω 48
ὑστερέω 60
ὑστέρημα 60
ὕστερος 60
ὑψηλός 60
ὕψιστος 60
ὕψος 60
ὑψόω 60

Φ

φαίνω 48
φανερός 48
φανερόω 48
φαῦλος 76
φείδομαι 71
φέρω 39
φεύγω 48
φημί 30
φθάνω 76
φθαρτός 64
φθείρω 64
φθόνος 76
φθορά 64
φιάλη 71
φιλαδελφία 48
φιλέω 48
φίλημα 48
φίλος 48
φλόξ 76
φοβέομαι 40
φόβος 40

φονεύς 60
φονεύω 60
φόνος 60
φορέω 40
φόρος 40
φορτίον 40
φρέαρ 76
φρονέω 49
φρόνιμος 49
φυλακή 49
φυλάσσω 49
φυλή 49
φύλλον 76
φύραμα 76
φυσιόω 76
φύσις 49
φυτεύω 49
φωνέω 31
φωνή 31
φῶς 40
φωτεινός 40
φωτίζω 40

Χ

χαίρω 25
χαλκός 76
χαρά 25
χάραγμα 77
χαρίζομαι 25
χάριν 25
χάρις 25
χάρισμα 25
χεῖλος 77
χειμών 77
χείρ 66
χειροποίητος 18
χείρων 71

χήρα 68
χιλίαρχος 33
χιλιάς 60
χίλιοι 60
χιτών 71
χοῖρος 71
χορτάζω 60
χόρτος 60
χράομαι 49
χρεία 49
χρήζω 49
χρῆμα 49
χρηματίζω 49
χρηστός 49
χρηστότης 49
χρίω 64
χρονίζω 49

χρόνος 49
χρυσίον 61
χρυσός 61
χρυσοῦς 61
χωλός 71
χώρα 49
χωρέω 49
χωρίζω 50
χωρίον 49
χωρίς 50

Ψ

ψάλλω 64
ψαλμός 64
ψεύδομαι 61
ψευδομαρτυρέω 36
ψεῦδος 61

ψευδοπροφήτης 61
ψεύστης 61
ψυχή 32
ψυχικός 32

Ω

ὦ 71
ὧδε 16
ᾠδή 64
ὥρα 66
ὡς 18
ὡσαννά 77
ὡσαύτως 18
ὡσεί 18
ὥσπερ 18
ὥστε 18
ὠφελέω 71